Grow Potent Marijuana, Cannabis & Weed Fast

The Ultimate Guide To Growing Weed Indoors & Outdoors For Beginners - Become An Expert In Horticulture, CBD Oil, Medical Marijuana & The Cannabis Business

John Lambkin

All.Copyrights.Reserved.

TABLE OF CONTENTS

INTRODUCTION 1

CHAPTER ONE : HISTORY, ORIGIN, AND BASIC KNOWLEDGE.. 8

CHAPTER TWO : CONTRADICTIONS AND MYTHS 16

CHAPTER THREE : INDOOR GROWING: HOW TO BEGIN.. 25

CHAPTER FOUR : INDOOR GROWING: SOWING & GERMINATION... 33

CHAPTER FIVE : INDOOR GROWING: PROPAGATION AND PLANTING TECHNIQUES.................................... 41

CHAPTER SIX : INDOOR GROWING: FLOWERING STAGE.. 49

CHAPTER SEVEN : OUTDOOR GROWING: FACTORS TO CONSIDER BEFORE STARTING 55

CHAPTER EIGHT : OUTDOOR GROWING: PLANTING TECHNIQUE AND PROPAGATION................................ 65

CHAPTER NINE : OUTDOOR GROWING: FLOWERING STAGE.. 71

CHAPTER TEN : NATURAL OR HUMAN PESTS IN MARIJUANA 80

CHAPTER ELEVEN : NUTRIENTS, MAINTENANCE, AND THE SOIL IN MARIJUANA.................................... 89

CHAPTER TWELVE : MARIJUANA HARVEST (INDOOR AND OUTDOOR GROWING) 97

CHAPTER THIRTEEN : MEDICAL MARIJUANA (HOW IT ALL BEGAN) 105

CHAPTER FOURTEEN : MEDICAL MARIJUANA
(EXPLORATION AND BREAK-THROUGH) 112

CHAPTER FIFTEEN : FROM BEGINNER TO EXPERT
GROWER (IT'S THAT EASY) 120

CONCLUSION 125

Introduction

Cannabis, cannabis, cannabis! Only very few of us wouldn't have heard about this psychoactive weed or herb. Irrespective of how many restrictions are placed on it by the governments of our various countries, it has still found a way of crossing borders and reaching our states, towns, cities, and streets.

A lot of us are of notion that this psychoactive weed is extremely harmful and addictive. We mostly believe that nothing good can come of cannabis consumption. This is a result of the heavy campaign levied against it by governments and other competing industries. However, the assumption they've fed you is not true. This Handbook will enlighten you and show you the benefits marijuana could give you as a grower and a consumer.

As a beginner, this Handbook will take you through an exciting phase which will enable you to become familiar with the guidelines that come with growing cannabis both indoor and outdoors. But rest assured, this book is committed to helping you become an expert grower in your own category.

At the end of this Handbook, you will be able to grow cannabis on your own, know which strains are best for which soil conditions, and know which nutrients (organic and inorganic) are best for the maintenance of your plants.

With cannabis painted black all over the world, this book will broaden your horizon along those myths and contradictions, thereby ensuring you are well-versed with the policies and enactments issued against the psychoactive herb.

Have you ever heard of medical marijuana? If not, there is no need to panic. This Handbook will go into detail and help you become conversant with its origin, development, and progress as of today. Nothing beats being knowledgeable in the details of your hobby.

Marijuana is sold in every nook and cranny of your city; you must have seen boys passing it around after taking a long drag, and also seen how its distributors shy away from the authorities. Instead of making up your mind about them, this Handbook will show you why such actions take place today.

You just don't bury the seeds on the ground; it's far more than that. It requires a process that is attributed to care, attention, tenderness, and carefulness. Growing marijuana is no joke. It might be tiring and stressful in the start, but trust me, the end result will be equally rewarding.

The chapters of this book will enlighten you and show you how you can become a great grower of the cannabis plant. Aside from that, the chapters are highly educative and informative. Chapter One looks at a brief history of the existence of the plant. How did it come into being? How was the cannabis plant discovered? Questions like these are answered in this chapter.

It is important to understand that, before starting anything, it would really help to know the historical background. We believe having knowledge about the history of the plant will give you the much-needed guidance toward caring for the plant. In the end, you will realize that cannabis is obviously one of the most beautiful, rare, and amazing plants planet earth holds.

Chapter Two clears up the contradictions and myths levied against this innocent plant. Thanks to the stereotypes propagated into society by some people who don't really share in the beneficial idea of cannabis, the plant's image has been soiled in the mud beyond recognition. You will learn the truth, thanks to the great advocates of the plants who never gave up the fight. This chapter will help open your eyes if you are a believer in those myths and stereotypes.

Chapter Three will be looking at how to begin growing your cannabis plant indoors. Cannabis growing is a sensitive activity, especially in areas where it is prohibited and criminalized. We will implore you to be very careful. Check the factors and balance the conditions so as to experience a stress-free and less strenuous cannabis growing venture.

The next chapter, Chapter Four basically shoulders the

sowing and germination process of growing cannabis. A lot of beginners end up making a mess of their gardens at this stage. You don't just bury the seeds; there are steps and rules to follow. There are guidelines that will help your seeds germinate at the appropriate time. Follow them in this chapter and there would be no cause for alarm.

And sometimes we just end up wanting more for our plants. We want our plants to exhibit the best qualities. We want our plants to grow plentifully. We want our plants to look healthy and possess great properties. This is where Chapter Five comes in. Propagation and planting techniques that will be discussed in this chapter will always come in handy.

Chapter Six will definitely look into the most sensitive phase of the cannabis plant life cycle; the flowering phase. What do you do in this particular phase? How do you trigger the phase? How do you care for the plants in their flowering phase? These questions and more are what this chapter will discuss. The flowering phase signals the end of the plant life cycle. In other words, it signals harvest.

Chapter Seven will be a start to another method of planting cannabis; the outdoor cannabis growing method. Before starting this method of cannabis growing, there are certain factors we should take into consideration. Outgrowing is blissful, but far riskier. Thus, one has to be extra careful to pull it off.

Chapter Eight also centers on the outdoor growing method for the cannabis plant. What is the best way to propagate the plant? What are the right techniques that will boost the plant in quality and quantity? If you want your plants to turn out well, then you really need to read through this chapter.

Chapter Nine focuses on the flowering stage of the outdoor plant. This is not like the indoor plant, which can be tweaked and triggered by the grower. As a matter of fact, the flowering stage of this plant can only be triggered naturally. So, why not read through it with rapt attention in order to know what to do when this stage comes?

All cannabis plants, both indoors and outdoors, have the tendency to carry diseases or even pests. These pests come in two forms - natural and human. What do we mean by a natural pest? What do we mean by a human pest? Want to find out? Then, read through Chapter Ten. It discusses the major pests you'd encounter and how to control these pests.

Chapter Eleven promises to be far more interesting, as it will look into the nutrients (natural and artificial), daily maintenance (indoors and outdoors), and the types of soil that are best for growing both indoor and outdoor cannabis plants. The three vital elements of light, air, and water will be discussed in this chapter. How do you maintain the fluorescent light in an indoor garden? What kind of fans are best to use and where should you place them? How much water do the plants need and does the soil hold?

The next chapter, Chapter Twelve will look into harvest in both methods of growing cannabis. Harvesting cannabis is far different and can be very stressful, especially in outdoor planting. How do you go about it? What do you need to do? What comes after clipping? These details and more are what this chapter will explain.

Chapter Thirteen will open your eyes to the term "medical marijuana." Medical marijuana is real; and in fact, one of the most advanced medicines in today's world. How did it begin? What is the historical background? How long has it been in existence? How long has marijuana been relevant in medicine? These and many more are the questions this chapter will tackle.

Chapter Fourteen puts the lid on medical marijuana. It will keep you abreast of the development and breakthroughs of the herb. You will be shocked to know in how many ways it has been useful to man ever since its legalization.

Then, the last chapter will quickly give you a recap of your journey from being the beginner that you are now to the expert you wish to become. It's no easy road, but if you follow this book sternly and to the letter, you will surely get there. That I can promise you.

To this effect, growing marijuana can be quite fun. A lot of people, especially those beginner and novice in growing marijuana, find it very difficult to maintain the plant – from sowing to harvest. It takes more than just having the intention to grow cannabis. Don't get me wrong - having the intention is also great. It's the first step to anything. But, before one can pull off growing a healthy cannabis plant, we need to ask ourselves these important questions:

1. **Are we ready?**

2. **Do we have what it takes?**

3. **Do we have time?**

Well, if your answers to all these questions are yes, then you are good to go. Be that as it may, we would implore you to take a deep breath. Clear your mind and be sure your attention is totally on this Handbook as you are about to start your journey from being a novice to an expert or professional in the line of marijuana growers.

Enjoy!

Chapter One

History, Origin, and Basic Knowledge

Just like every other plant, weed, or even herb, marijuana started out long before man discovered it. It began as a stray plant in the midst of other different kinds of plants. Sometimes, it grows out in small groups in places man wouldn't even know it could grow, and in severe weather conditions man didn't know it could survive.

These ancestral marijuana plants were grown not by man, but by a combination of different dispersing agents. Over and over again, they would germinate and be sown, either by hard, whirling winds that carried the seeds far and wide, luckily attached to the hooves of cattle or other groups of animals traveling from one place to another, or even attached to the beaks of birds when pecking the hard soil for their prey.

This process has continuously been in motion as marijuana growth spread all over the Earth. Man discovered the plant long before the Reformation period, though no one can actually put a date on when he first started using marijuana. History has it that marijuana originated from Asia, mostly China, Mongolia, and Southern Siberia, before reaching out to other countries of the world as time went on.

With a history of over 12,000 years of existence, the

cannabis plant can be said to be one of the world's oldest plants. Archeologists and researchers have found old, frail, burnt seeds of the cannabis plant at the Kurgan Burial Mounds in Siberia. These seeds are argued to be thousands of years old, dating to approximately 3000 BC.

Some seeds were also found in the tombs of the nobles buried in some regions of China. These seeds are nothing but extremely effective psychoactive marijuana seeds. Thus, if the people of this era had smoked the marijuana plant, that should tell you how ancient the marijuana plant - and its use - really is.

Little by little, marijuana became the lasting medicine to man problems. When ancient medicine men discovered the plant, they didn't know the plant would be so very versatile in curing many diseases all at once. This discovery gave rise to its popularity. However, it was widely known that marijuana could be used for more than just smoking.

For instance, in the 20th century, marijuana was widely used for making a strong kind of fabric which had proven to be more durable than, and stand the test of time better than other fibers. That is just one of the many things this versatile psychoactive herb can be used for.

Many years down the line, scientists and researchers became aware of the many medical benefits of the cannabis plant. This discovery has revolutionized the face of marijuana from that of a rebel to that of a savior. As W. B. Campbell rightly put it in his 1914 *Handbook of Modern Treatment and Medical Formulary*,

"Cannabis is highly recommended for the following diseases: bronchitis, cancer, corns, coryza, cough, headache, impotence, prostatitis, strangury, warts, whooping cough, Opium habit, migraine, menorrhagia, gastralgia, dyspepsia, and so much more.

In the same way we have broken down the origin of cannabis, don't you think it would make sense if we seek to understand what cannabis itself entails? As far as we know, it might be anything whatsoever. But so far, you would deduce from our earlier discussion that cannabis is a psychoactive plant or herb, as the case may be.

But in truth, cannabis is much more than just a plant or herb. To some people, it is life itself. To some, it is their companion in times of grief, depression, and solitude. To some, it is a hobby which they can never give up as it comes with a rewarding end. And to others, it is the only connection they've felt with friends and fellow users of the plant. Nevertheless, what is cannabis, really?

What is Cannabis?

Aside from the Moringa leaf that also seems to have a multipurpose use, no other plant possesses the outstanding qualities and purposes the cannabis plant does. The cannabis plant is beautiful, purposeful, and one of the most interesting plants one can grow. It grows even in the harshest of weather; it improves soil PH & nutrients; and it provides man with fuel, flowers, pleasure, food, and most importantly, medicine.

It can be grown outdoors, or even indoors, as the case may be. It all depends on the method that suits your preference. But rest assured, both are exceedingly successful in their growth. Thankfully, you don't need to hide while growing the cannabis plant in parts of the United States. All thanks to the recent laws supporting the freedom attached to growing and using the cannabis plant, gone are the days one would need to be extremely careful when doing so.

Right now, most parts of the country have legalized the use of the plant. However, it is still labeled "a harmful substance" in many countries of the world. Issues revolving around it are dealt with harsh penalties and conditions. To this effect, if you are still in a country where the laws of the land don't support cannabis growth or usage, we would implore you to stick to the traditional way of growing – growing while staying conscious.

Botanically, the cannabis plant is one hell of a plant, with three distinctive species. These species are the Sativa (which is the popular species of cannabis you would likely find around), the Indica (which is also popular but not as popular as the Sativa), and the Ruderalis (which is not really popular like the Sativa and the Indica species).

Additionally, many botanists have argued about the classification of these species of the cannabis plant. They argued that the plant is generally a Sativa kind of species, with two distinctive subspecies of Sativa, which are Indica and Ruderalis, respectively.

The cannabis plant is tall and straight, with leaves and branches spreading all over the stem in the shape of a Christmas tree. Its flower (mostly Indica) possesses a strong, thick, foul smell - which is widely referred amongst users of the plants as "skunk." Also, only the Sativa and Indica species have a high amount of THC (Tetrahydrocannabinol). The Ruderalis, on the other hand, has a small amount of THC.

Cannabis Properties and Varieties

It is important to know that the cannabis plant possesses great properties which lots of people from all walks of find useful to them. Like the saying goes, "What is good for the goose is also perfect for the gander." If the THC content of the cannabis plant is perfect enough to provide the right inspiration and creativity for an artist while stroking his brush, it can also be perfect for a workaholic who wants a clear mind at the end of the day.

Cannabis properties as an intoxicant are greatly and immensely respected by anyone who has an idea of what it contains. The rise and advancements in the breeding of the cannabis plant have taken the creation of different strains in the species to a whole new level. Breeders now know exactly what species and strains to crossbreed to accomplish the result they want.

The introduction of crossbreeding opens the doors to a new dawn in the breeding of the cannabis plant. This has given birth to many new strains. The new greenhouse technology allows breeders to grow their strains at a specific timeline of their choosing. This can be achieved by the manipulation of the cannabis plant's features or qualities this technology offers.

To this effect, the growing of the cannabis plant in the modern world can be attributed to just a few reasons - for medical use, and for a recreational purpose. Therefore, growers that are more aligned with the medical benefits of the plant should grow more of an Indica species. It has the ability to help you feel calm and relaxed; it can even induce a good sleep, and so much more.

For growers who are also aligned toward the recreational usage and activities of the cannabis plant, we would recommend you start growing the Sativa species. It is highly characterized by an enormous amount of THC, which is synonymous with creative and physical energy creation. This brings us to the question - what exactly is THC?

What is THC?

We cannot discuss marijuana without mentioning this abbreviation. As a matter of fact, a weed without THC can be referred to be a vegetable. A weed without THC is like a train without an engine. THC, which is the short-term for tetrahydrocannabinol, is a psychoactive, psychotomimetic, or as the case may be, an intoxicating content in the cannabis plant.

The amount of THC in different species of the cannabis plant varies. THC is produced in the trichrome and resin glands, which are located at the lower part of the plant. The THC content in each plant determines the potency. Therefore, if you want to grow your cannabis plant, we would implore you to keep this in mind. How heavy do you want your plants to be in THC? Are you growing cannabis just for its medicinal purposes, or for recreational pleasure?

Aside from THC, there are lots of cannabinoids present in the plant. According to research, there are over sixty identified cannabinoids in a cannabis plant. Some of them are as follows; cannabigerol (CBG), cannabichromene (CBC), cannabidiol

(CBD), cannabicyclol (CBL), canmabielsion (CBE), cannabidiol (CBND), cannabitriol (CBT), and so many more.

However, a cannabis plant possesses more THC and cannabidiol (CBD) than any other cannabinoids. The new trend of checking the rates of potency in the cannabis plant is now being attributed to the high mix of various cannabinoids, and not just THC levels.

That and more are what the origin and characteristics of the plant entail. It is no wonder how this highly medicinal plant, if fully utilized, would be more a blessing to man than a curse which has been soiled down in the mud. How has it been given a bad name? How has it been attributed so many contradictions and myths? These topics and more are what we will be discussing in our next chapter. You won't want to miss it!

Chapter Two

Contradictions and Myths

Daniel, who is a twenty-two-year-old sophomore, has been involved with an ongoing court case. His crime? He had been caught with a whole parcel of weed which he had been carrying in his school bag all day long. According to him, he had planned on meeting with friends to distribute the weed among them.

Daniel revealed that he smokes weed every day, as it helps him move past his stress and anxiety problems. Even with his heavy smoking routine, he had maintained an outstanding GPA of 3.6. Also, Daniel hadn't smoked weed ever since he had been caught, over the span of twenty-one days. He seems to be perfectly fine and sane. As a matter of fact, he has said he is more than ready to go through a dope test and therapy.

Now, the questions we all should ask ourselves are: Are these misconceptions about marijuana really accurate? Since many have claimed that the marijuana plant is a harmful herb, why didn't it harm Daniel? Why isn't Daniel addicted to the potency and thrill of the marijuana?

Daniel's case would make you realize that the cannabis plant is more of a help than poison to not just Daniel but every other user you'd find. Despite the fact that he smokes every day, he still manages an impressive GPA of 3.6. The marijuana plant also helped him solve his anxiety and stress problems overnight. Would you still say the cannabis plant has been harmful to Daniel in any way whatsoever?

The answer is no. In fact, it has made Daniel a better version of himself. He didn't become an addict; instead, it helped him become more calm. He didn't become a failure in school; rather he maintained a very impressive performance. The cannabis plant gave him solace and peace of mind; something he cannot buy anywhere in the market with money.

There is no better measure of the immense uses and purposes of the marijuana plant if only we learn to accept it and change our negative opinion about it. That is the only way we will see the good this plant is actually capable of doing.

According to Barney Warf, "The idea that this is an evil drug is a very recent construction, and the fact that it is illegal is a historical anomaly."

These misconceptions and myths about the cannabis plant have been woven over the years to suit the narrative of the opposing side. Many of us had been brainwashed so badly that when we hear of the words "weed," "cannabis," "skunk," "pot," "marijuana," "dope," "MJ," and more, the only thing that comes to our minds is the picture of the haggardlylooking ragamuffins found in the dirtiest corners of our streets, distributing poison to the young population.

This is a total misconception and it is not true. As a matter of fact, it is a complicated way of thinking in regards to marijuana. It is the picture these opposing forces have painted in our minds.

In the United States, the introduction of the plant in different parts of the country has influenced various sectors like agriculture, medicine, recreation, and religion. The first American president, George Washington had also laid emphasis on the plant as regards its use for fabric production.

He believed hemp was the new fiber that would revolutionize the fabric-making industry with its strong, thick, and durable texture. It is believed to be three times better than normal cotton and wool, thus, would go a long way in saving the common man money on clothes.

This wide acceptance of the plant was short-lived as Harry Anslinger led a crusade on rendering marijuana growth and usage illegal. He and many others believed that the marijuana plant was capable of leading man to insanity, which in turn would make the users of the plant commit criminal acts. In 1936, Anslinger and his believers made a breakthrough as there were restrictions and bans placed on the psychoactive herb all over the country.

But guess what? Anslinger didn't stop there. He heavily lobbied for the Marijuana Tax Act, which was passed in 1937. This was aimed toward restricting the sale and use of the plant in the everyday lives of Americans. Little by little, marijuana was pushed out of society, with various campaigns programmed to achieve their aim.

The straw that broke the camel's back was the release of the popular movie "Reefer Madness" in 1936. The movie was aimed at sowing the seeds of negativity in the minds of Americans - and guess what? It worked like magic. People started growing negative thoughts about marijuana plants. They began to fear the plant as something dangerous that could cause them insanity.

They now started seeing smokers of the herb as having the tendency to become unstable, violent, and even dangerous. With all that's been portrayed over the years, it is important to know that the uses, purposes, and effectiveness of the marijuana plant didn't change at all. It still remains the same herb with the same advantages and disadvantages. This contradiction has now passed down from generation to generation.

It has eaten deed to the extent that even the positive side of the herb still can't overshadow this contradiction. These stereotypes even evolved into a generalization. The use of marijuana is now being attributed to certain tribes, ethnic groups, cultures, and religions. For example, rap artists, African Americans, Mexican Americans, and other groups are being stereotyped every blessed day of their lives as chain-smokers of the plant.

Be that as it may, these well-woven narratives and stereotypes have done more harm than good. However, the birth of a new millennia ushered in a fresh perspective and view of the marijuana plant. Movements were organized, protests were staged, and laws were enacted.

Finally, the bill that stamped the ban on the use and growing of the cannabis plant fell through in the late 90s and early 2000. As a result, lots of states and regions under the United States started enacting laws that support the freedom to use and grow the plant. One tool used in the fight for freedom of the use and growth of the cannabis plant is the media.

Advocates of this perception took the social media world by storm with hashtags on Twitter, Facebook, and Instagram trending all over the country. The fight for legalizing marijuana became quite popular, with lots of people supporting the train as it moved toward a better future for users and breeders.

Well, with what we are looking at and events churning up, one can say the freedom of the users and breeders of the cannabis plant might be a debatable discussion all over again. In 2013, the Monitoring the Future Data research which is carried out by researchers at the University of Michigan continuously raised the hopes of marijuana becoming banned and restricted all over again.

According to annual research focusing on the use of drugs and alcohol in today's youth, there has been a troubling increase in the use of drugs and alcohol by the youth of today, thus, giving room for a second thought in the freedom that comes with those laws guiding cannabis growth and use.

This research might be true, but it is important to know that judging the marijuana plant can be quite confusing, especially with our emotions getting the better of us. We cannot fully accept the possibility of the plant if we keep getting sensitive each time we hear about marijuana.

Many of us end up painting the plant red before hearing anything about it. We focus our minds into hating weed as a social skunk that eats our sanity. Additionally, we let our personal experiences with the psychoactive herb get in the way of our understanding. For example, a person who has finally managed to stay clean and sober from marijuana would definitely not paint a good picture of the plant.

He or she would not mention the usefulness, purposefulness, and outstanding attributes of the marijuana plant - but instead, continuously mention how he or she became a shadow of his or her self. You can't start saying things about the plant today when the last time you smoked one was in the 60s, or even 50s. There is a long gap between the 60s, and now and a lot has happened over that period.

Today's marijuana issue is quite different and evolved. There are high risks that come with the drug as well as adequate safety nets. Marijuana is not addictive. It doesn't have the power to make one addicted.

The story of Daniel is a very good example. However, it is one's choice to become addicted or not. The potency of the plants (cannabinoids) cannot really hold you to keep coming back for more. Although they are quite intoxicating, the power to become an addict lies with you. Addiction is a choice.

Myths about Marijuana

1. Marijuana is harmful. This is the kind of message campaigns like Reefer Madness, Monitoring the Future Data, and many more have passed and are still passing to date. Though this myth might come with a little bit of truth, the way and manner in which it is being propagated are wrong and absolutely demeaning.

This myth has been supported by many research papers and experiments. Marijuana is not harmful if you control your use. As a matter of fact, it can even be more of a help to you than a burden. Let's say I smoke a wrap of weed twice a week. That is very normal and under control. But smoking two to three wraps every day can be quite crazy and out of hand.

Medically, there have been no implications of harmful effects of the plant to the body. In fact, it has been tipped to be highly medicinal and cures almost every sickness and disease. The fear of this psychoactive drug starts when people begin to associate the end result of weed intake to madness. It is wrong and absolutely incorrect. Not all psychiatric patients are suffering from too much marijuana intake.

2. Marijuana leads to addiction. I have said this before and I will say it again, having total control of how and when you take or smoke in cannabis is totally your choice. It is your choice to smoke it ten times a day or once every week. Thus, marijuana doesn't have the power to make you addicted.

This is a myth that has been widely misconstrued by lots of people over time. It all depends on our power and will to smoke the plant. A man who is suffering from depression would easily find his best friend and solace in the hands of marijuana. Equally, a man who is perfectly alright psychologically would know when and how to take marijuana just for pleasure.

You can see the difference between these two people. One is a homeless person looking for the light and the other is just a man hoping to while away his time. Addiction is a choice. We all have this power. It just depends on the situation we all find ourselves in.

The fight for freedom as regards cannabis has been an on and off kind of situation. With the recent call for its ban and restriction, it's only a matter of time before the relevant authorities take this up with iron hands. But before that happens, let's make you into the best grower you can be.

Chapter Three

Indoor Growing: How to Begin

Growing Marijuana is an interesting venture or activity. Some people even call it a hobby. It involves the thorough and complete care and attention focused on the plant from its sowing stage to the harvest. It is indeed a hobby, after all. If you don't have the passion for growing this psychoactive weed, then we would suggest you don't even waste your time at all.

Can you really spare time for this plant? Can you maintain and take good care of the plant - and not by proxy? Do you really have what it takes to grow one? Are you really sure you want to venture into that?

If you can answer all these questions with a yes, then we see no reason why you shouldn't give growing cannabis a chance. You might often wonder where your friends end up getting the best and most unique weed you've ever smoked. When you ask them, the natural thing they will tell you is that they bought it from their vague distributor or something. That is their way of putting you off. They are probably growing weed in a corner of their house if you look closely.

So do you want to be left behind? Wouldn't you rather join their train of the expedition and grow your own preference of weed? Growing weed is very simple if you get the necessary factors on your side. One can't just wander off to start a cannabis farm either indoors or outdoors, especially in a country or region where the laws of the land still negate growing it.

To this effect, staying on top of your game is paramount. One needs to adopt the indoor growing system of the cannabis plant, which gives you at least 50% security from the prying eyes of the law. Imagine trying to grow the cannabis plant anywhere in Africa. This is a continent known for its rich cultural heritage, beliefs, and values.

You can't just wake up one day in Africa and start tilling the soil and growing some weed anywhere you want. Most nations of Africa, if not all, still see the cannabis plant as a harmful substance which must be eliminated in the streets and corners of their country. Thus, you will need to be very careful with the way you go about it, so as not to be arrested for engaging in the hobby.

Therefore, knowing all this, it is also important for us to know that there are mitigating factors that may or may not turn the tides of growing cannabis successfully in our favor. The success rate of our plants rests entirely on our shoulders. How many steps have we taken to ensure successful growth and harvest? How did we end up going about it?

It gets to a point where these questions will be very important in our quest to grow cannabis. Trust me, you will feel nervous and scared scared; anxiety might even set in. Do not panic, because this is very normal. This is obviously your first time trying something of this nature, especially for those in prohibited countries or regions. What if everything goes wrong? What if I can't keep up? What if I eventually get caught?

Questions like this will fill our minds. But trust me, you are not going to get caught. Besides, you aren't doing anything wrong; instead, you are only doing what you love and have a passion for. So, clear your mind of those negative thoughts. This is obviously why you are reading this Handbook in the first place. We are here to guide you positively.

Be that as it may, we would want you to know that one secret weapon that has been very useful to expert growers of the cannabis plant is the ability to keep their mouths shut. Being secretive is the ingredient you need to pull this off. No one should know you are growing the cannabis plant in your house except yourself.

In this line of business, hobby, or even activity, no one can be trusted. If you are traveling out of town, for example, and you need someone to look after your plant, be sure its someone you know inside and out. - someone that would never think of selling you out. And when you've eventually harvested your plant, you might want to share with friends.

Even when they ask you where you get that kind of strain, never tell them you are growing it in your room. Tell them exactly what they want to hear. And that is that you are buying it from a new distributor in town. That should seal their mouths from asking further questions.

In order to pull off a successful indoor cannabis farm, there are factors that need to be checked, balanced, and checkmated before embarking on the path. You can't just set out on this path without the necessary things to help you navigate the obstacles and problems you will definitely encounter on your way to harvest.

Here are the factors that need to be met before embarking on growing the cannabis plant indoors.

1. **Geographical Location:** This is one hell of a mitigating factor. Like we said earlier, you can't just wake up one morning and start tilling the soil. You really need to take the climate condition of the environment into consideration. Where is the geographical location? How well is it secured? Is it really secluded from prying eyes? Is your grow room big enough? Can it withhold the smell, especially during the flowering stage?

These are questions that need to be answered correctly. For example, what if your utility bills suddenly shoot up above normal with the high amount of water, light, and so on that you would need? Won't the authorities come knocking on your door? What relevant steps have you taken to ensure that the incident would be checkmated?

The geographical location matters a lot when growing your plant. Many expert growers even go far away from the city in order to grow their plants successfully. We would recommend you do this if you really don't have the right place to use. Especially if you can't get a medical marijuana permit.

2. **Security**: This is the heart of every venture, business or activity. If you really want to pull off growing cannabis indoors, you must put in place the right security. If your plants end up growing too high and reach the windows, where every passersby can see their leaves or flowers, what will you do?

Everything needs to be in its appropriate manner. You need to be sure that your grow room isn't just available to anybody and everybody that enters into your home. It needs to be tightly secured. Like we discussed above, growing marijuana should be your secret. You wouldn't want your friends or foes get hold of the information, would you? In this line of hobby, anyone and everyone can not be trusted.

Security is paramount, especially for those in countries or regions where growing cannabis is an offense. Imagine a plumber comes in to check your pipes and sewage. Imagine him taking a walk in and out of your house at that moment. Better still, imagine an official inspector comes in to inspect the house for insects or pests. What would you do?

How tightly secured is your grow room? Does it hold the foul smell? Or can the next door neighbor smell it?

3. **Know the Numbers:** I would say it is important for you to know that growing indoors has to deal with the number of plants you want to grow. You can't expect to grow the same number of the cannabis plants you'd be able to grow outdoors, while indoors. The outdoors has unlimited space while the indoors are just limited to the four corners of your room.

Most indoor growers are growing the cannabis plant for mostly personal use. Thus, the number of plants they may want to grow would be quite small. This will give you the exact idea of how big your grow room should be. Is it just a couple of pots? Or a dozen of them? Know the answers to these questions and you are good to go.

4. **Financial Constraints:** All businesses are attributed to this factor. So, are you growing cannabis as a business venture or just a hobby. How much are you willing to spend? What is your considered budget? These are

questions we should ask ourselves before choosing the method of growing we want to use.

An indoor growing method can be quite expensive to pull off. Trust me, I know exactly how it feels when you bring out money from your pocket to purchase the things Mother Nature would provide for you on a free of charge basis if you opted for the outdoor growing method.

It can be quite a lot sometimes. For example, you would have to buy a good and steady fluorescent light for your indoor garden while the sun shines brightly in the outdoor garden. It is very normal for you to start thinking about your pocket along this line. Removing air, soil, light, water, and so much more from your budget would do wonders to your pockets.

So ask yourself if you are really ready to go down this lane. And if you are, then there is nothing stopping you from growing your cannabis indoors.

5. **Kinds of Strains You Want to Grow:** Some strains are better off indoors than outdoors. They tend to grow better, faster, and perfectly well indoors. Indoor plants tend to be more easily influenced than those outdoor. For example, the grower might decide when to switch off the lights more in order to foster the flowering

stage. The grower might also be able to easily tweak the strains to his or her preference.

This is why many growers of the cannabis plant go for this method. The strains are created to withstand these adaptations. They are programmed to focus on being flexible with their traits. Many cannabis growers like these particular strains, and end up going for the indoor growing. Therefore, if the indoor strains possess the kinds of traits you want, then it would give you no choice but to opt for this method of growing cannabis.

In starting any hobby, passion, or even business, the first thing to tackle is always how to begin. How do we go about making sure this thing we are venturing into turns out to be a success? How much effort have we put in place to ensure everything comes out perfectly?

If we can successfully tackle these key factors and find answers to them, then there is nothing stopping us from starting our cannabis farm. This book will further take you through the processes and techniques that will be useful to you as you aim to become one hell of an expert grower.

Chapter Four

Indoor Growing: Sowing & Germination

Sowing any seeds goes beyond burying them and then forgetting to dig up those particular seeds. Like we pointed out earlier, the origin of marijuana began with its seeds being dispersed by the wind, marching cattle, or birds pecking the ground for food. It is important to know that sowing the cannabis seed also entails techniques.

You can't just go about digging up the soil anywhere you want. There are procedures you follow for that to happen, in order for your sowed seed to germinate properly. After getting the right geographical location, putting in place adequate security, and ensuring a well-ventilated and spacious grow room, sowing your seed becomes the next thing to do.

Sowing the seed boils down to choosing the kind of strain you want. Like we pointed out in the previous chapter, there are basically three species of the cannabis plant you can choose from, and each of them has a wide number of strains breeders of the plant have created over time.

To this effect, if you care more about your plants having a high level of cannabinoids, then there are various strains for that. If you want a plant with long, wide leaves which will, in turn, leave you with a bumper harvest, then those kinds of strains are also available. The choice of strains is endless.

You can even get the much-needed seeds from friends who are breeders or an online seed bank. We would recommend you go for the online banks because they often have lots of varieties and strains you are able to choose from.

After carefully sowing the seeds with the right soil and procedures, the next thing is to wait for them to germinate. Germination comes a few days after sowing. A new plant will begin to sprout out from the seed you buried deep in the soil. This germination process can also be called "popping."

The color of the seeds determines how potent they will be when you sow them. Many beginners don't know this and they will end up buying something that is worthless and will not germinate in the long run. Go for something that looks mature, with a very dark brown color, light accents, and a very hard touch. This is the best kind of seed you will find around. If the seeds look fresh and all green, it's a sign of the seeds being immature.

After getting the kinds of seeds you want to grow, getting the right soil becomes really paramount. Some indoor breeders or growers with a low budget will choose getting natural soil directly from the ground. This is very acceptable, so long the soil is highly nutritious.

You can also get great quality soil that is well-packaged

and sold at any agricultural soil close to you. There are lots of great soils you will find handy. For example, the Miracle-Gro Moisture Control Garden Soil has a great combination of the NPK (Nitrogen, Phosphorus, and Potassium). With that being said, we should ask ourselves this important question: how can we really sow the cannabis seed perfectly?

Aside from getting your soil with the necessary nutrients they need, the seeds also need three key elements to survive. Without these elements, they would probably stay buried in the soil forever, without even sprouting. Just like any other plant you know, they also need water, sunlight, and most importantly, air. Without these three elements, cannabis seeds will not grow indoors.

Get a grow pot; then fill in the pot with the soil. You have to a considerable amount. Sowing the soil comes next. Many people make the mistake of dipping the seeds too far underground. They tend to dig too deep when sowing their seeds. This has repercussions as the seeds might find it hard to sprout.

Some might even end up not growing at all. When sowing the seeds, we shouldn't dig too deep or too shallow. That way, the plant can get enough sunlight, air, and water for it to properly germinate.

Now, this is the best part of sowing the cannabis seeds -

the waiting part. Knowing full well that you have successfully sowed your seed with the right soil, waiting for it to sprout is the next thing to do. This period might be filled with tense moments and situations. Trust me, as it's your first time, it can be worrisome.

What if it doesn't sprout? What if you've made a mistake when sowing? What if the water, air, and sunlight just aren't enough? These random questions will definitely start going through your mind. Don't panic if the seeds don't sprout in the first few days. Some seeds might take more time to sprout. Like we pointed out above, it all depends on how deep you bury your seeds.

The sowed seeds gradually open up in the soil and begin to sprout. This single sprout it will come out with is called the taproot. It is what every grower of cannabis would want to see after sowing their seeds. It's what indicates successful germination of your seeds. Don't get too carried away as it is your first time growing the cannabis plant.

You might want to start touching it out of curiosity. Please don't; they are not too strong and can be very fragile. Thus, be careful so they do not break off. Make sure there is nothing competing with your taproot. For example, clear out anything that may cause any problems to the growth of the plant.

Indoor sowing of the cannabis plant is quite easy and less

stressful compared to outdoors. Instead of a large area of land where we would have to start getting worried about tilling, weeding, and so much more, the indoor method of growing cannabis offers us with a limited area or grow room.

With just a very good lighting condition, a well-ventilated window or even a standby fan, and a well-irrigated water system, your indoor grow room will be all set. This is why we recommend you go for this method of growing.

And in case you want to transplant your tap roots, that is also possible. Transplanting is the transportation or movement of your plant or even tap root from one soil or pot to another as the case may be. First, get a similar pot of about 2 inches, then ensure that it is filled with enough soil. Use something strong, and long, but narrow to make a small quarter inch hole.

Then, carefully transfer the seeds from their original place of germination to the new pot. Please don't use your hands to carry the seed. Instead, use tweezers to pick up the seed with the sprouted leaf facing up. Then, gently and carefully cover the hole with the soil.

Please don't forget to water it occasionally. Here, we would recommend you try using a spray bottle so as to keep the soil moist. It's true that the seeds need water, but that doesn't mean they should be soaked in water. This will definitely kill the seeds as they are still not well matured.

Keep a steady temperature, air, water, and sunlight level at all times for a week, after which your seeds will now begin to sprout seedlings from beneath the soil. But, rest assured, the rapid growth and pop-out of the seed are solely determined by the strains you chose. While some are slow and eventually take lots of time before they begin sprouting, others are just very fast when it comes to sprouting seedlings.

Ways Of Germinating Seeds (Transplanting)

1. **The Seed Soil Propagation:** This is one of the best propagation methods that can be used when germinating the seeds. Instead of using a cloth, towel, or even paper, actual soil can only be used here. Thus, this can be quite difficult but very efficient. Here, the seeds are to be placed in a hole in the soil, dug about 3mm deep, which is equivalent to the length of the cannabis seed when placed on the ground upright.

The soil should be moist and not in any way hard. It also should not be too wet for the seeds to germinate perfectly and at the right time. Thus, water should only be applied to it via a spray bottle once a day, or maybe twice. Do this continuously until the seeds start germinating. However, not all seeds will survive.

2. **Seed Towel Propagation**: Here, there is no need for soil as the seeds are being placed inside a wet or dampened towel. Any kind of towel can be used; cotton, wool, or even cheesecloth. The towel must be kept moist and not too wet at all times so as not to destroy the seeds.

Be sure to check the seeds every day to make sure they are in good condition. And if you sense any form of germination (tap root), it is very advisable for you to immediately transfer them to a much better condition - in a grow pot with the best quality soil. Do not touch them with your hands as that can render them useless.

Use a pair of tweezers for this purpose. Sometimes, growers end up losing their seeds as the transplanting process comes with glitches. Be very careful and swift in transplanting the seeds. If it happens to you, don't feel bad. Trust me, with time, you will get better.

3. **Rockwool SBS Tray Propagation:** This is obviously the best method growers use in germinating their cannabis seeds. Though it may be old-fashioned, it is obviously the best method used thus far. The Rockwool SBS tray will be soaked in water for a long time until it dampens.

After this, you will place the seeds in it and await germination. It is important to know that the Rockwool SBS tray can hold water for a long time, thus setting you free from the stress of watering the seeds daily. Getting the Rockwool SBS tray should be quite easy as you can either order it online or find it in any agricultural store near you.

Sowing goes beyond just burying the seeds. It includes several other techniques, just as we have pointed out above. Now, the choice is yours as to which germination technique is perfect for you. Mind you, any one you choose is very effective and efficient. However, some would definitely prove to be much more effective than others. And when your seeds do not germinate fast or even germinate at all, do not panic. It happens to everyone.

Chapter Five

Indoor Growing: Propagation and Planting Techniques

In the previous chapters, we discussed how to start growing the plant. True to our words, getting the intention to grow should be the first thing to make up in your mind, after which other things can follow suit. You don't expect someone who is not totally committed toward the growth of the plant to start growing it in his or her room.

Well, allow us to congratulate you on the first step to growing a healthy cannabis plant. Now that your plant has germinated, what's next? Are you going to continue taking care of it, or just let it grow by itself? Are you going to change the pot or just leave it exactly where it started sprouting? Are you going to apply sophisticated techniques to make it grow perfectly, or just leave everything in the hands of nature?

Growing indoors allows you to become the influencer of nature in your own way. For example, you can decide to get a very sophisticated lighting condition which will help the plant grow rapidly. You can also get a perfect working air conditioning machine to enable the plant to absorb more air. These are activities you can engage yourself in as you try to influence the growth of the plant.

What is Indoor Propagation?

You can also turn the tides in your favor by engaging in various planting techniques. Your slow-growing plants can now become healthier and bigger. Propagation, on the other hand, helps your plants multiply in folds. It is procreation for the cannabis plant. Instead of getting new seeds, which may cause additional stress, why not just create offspring from the original seeds.

These offspring would hold almost 80 to 90 percent features of the parent seed. Don't get it twisted, propagation is the real process of growing in the cannabis field, even if most expert growers out there treat it like it's just some step which is compulsory to get the right combination of strains.

Engaging in propagation comes with tough choices. For example, one might begin to ask himself if growing all the seeds bought would be a good idea. We might also ask ourselves if removing the male plants and leaving the females to thrive or uprooting the females and leaving the males in order to gain more mixed strains is a good idea. It all depends on how well and how much you want to grow your plant.

If your plan is to get mixed offspring (more than seeds) from the male plants, then we would recommend you uproot the females afterward. But, if you are more focused on getting the best psychoactive substance out of the plants, then the males should go. It all depends on your preference.

Many breeders of the cannabis plant look at lots of preferences available at their disposal before breeding for the exact kind of traits they want. They may want the breed to make sure it includes any of these qualities:

1. **High level of cannabinoids**

2. **Hardiness**

3. **Vigor and strength**

4. **Large and green leaves**

5. **Pest and disease resistance**

6. **High-quality seeds**

7. **Pleasant flower smell**

8. **Great taste, and so much more.**

Every breeder wants many, if not all, of these qualities in their breed and these can only be achieved via propagation. Here are some ways to propagate your plants.

Cloning

Have you ever heard of cloning? Well, you must have heard about humans cloning themselves or even software ways you can clone applications or even the whole content of a device. Well, in this sense, cloning can also be said to copy the features and strains of a particular seed, thereby producing an offspring that will contain those qualities. What you germinate is exactly what you will get in return.

Most breeders end up cloning due to the fact that they want to get a higher number of the female plant than the male. It entails taking part of the mother plant (possibly female) and planting it separately in a grow space for germination. Cloning is not as easy as it sounds. It's a big decision you should take your time making because it comes with its own share of heavy disasters.

For example, there is no improved version of the plant at all. As a matter of fact, the plant maintains the same kind of genotype and strain as the mother plant. Also, if one plant is affected by a disease, the other clones would be easily affected, as well. It's more like a one for all, all for one kind of situation.

Thus, having more than one clone plant in your garden is very advisable. That way, there would not be an entire garden of identical plants which are of the same mother plant. To this effect, if a disease breaks out on the plants, only the ones of the same genotype and traits would be affected. That would not automatically be a loss of all the plants on your own end.

When cloning, do not cut the part of the plant recklessly or abnormally. This might cause an injury to the plant, which would end up damaging it. Cut out the part swiftly and neatly.

Do not allow the detached part to stay too long before planting it in the soil. Naturally, all plants try to heal themselves immediately after they are injured. Thus, too much delay might render the detached part rather useless and damaged.

Be sure to get all the necessary tools and resources in order to pull this off perfectly. If you are thinking you would just use your hand to break off a part, then you are completely wrong. This might work, but its chances are really low when compared with the due process of cloning. Cloning is the perfect way to multiply your strains.

What are Indoor Planting Techniques?

Like we pointed out earlier in this chapter, growers of the plant apply planting techniques so as to get a happy result in the long run. When your plants are growing abnormally, getting worried would be a natural thing to do, especially after pouring your time, energy, and attention into it. We now begin to think of ways in which we would be able to salvage our plants. This is where planting techniques come in.

Planting techniques are advanced methods one can apply to his or her garden of weed as time progresses. These advanced methods come in handy so as to breed a healthy, good-looking weed. Now the question remains, what are these techniques and when do we need to apply these them?

1. **Topping:** Topping off the plants at a certain stage of growth can help improve the strength, taste, and yield of them. This involves cutting or breaking off a part of the plant, mostly the top part of it. According to expert growers, this will enable the plant to concentrate its nutrients on not just the top part but also other vital parts of the plant, thereby producing more than one cola in the long run.

Thus, instead of the plant continuing to focus on growing tall and high in a vertical manner, it would start getting thicker, thereby giving it more strength to withstand any external threats. Topping is also preferred by a lot of growers because it is quite easy to pull off. Now, where do you cut off when it comes to topping?

According to expert growers, topping is only possible if you cut the newest branch attached to the main stem neatly and nicely. Please do not use your hands in performing this function. Instead, use your cutting tool. The end result will see your plant becoming much fuller and bigger.

2. **SOG (Sea of Green):** The SOG is a planting technique that will leave a smile on the face of every indoor cannabis grower. Instead of thinning and throwing out the unwanted females, how about you clone them in a different grow room, know as SOG grow room?

First of all, the SOG technique can only be applied at the flowering stage of all species. That way, it will be very easy to pull through since it's close to the harvest period. Take as many clones as you deem fit because the SOG techniques lie in the wideness and deepness of the grow pot.

SOG got its name as a result of the way these clones arrange themselves in the grow room, forming an exact same height and growth pattern which would the top in form of a sea of greens if you are looking at it from above It's going to be a bumper harvest for you.

3. **SCROG (Screen of Greens):** This is a replica of the SOG, except with the inclusion of a screen being attached closely to the light. The screen will stand as the intermediary between your light and the plants. It is made out of wire mesh. What does this barricade do? It's simple.

Just like the SOG technique, the SCROG also needs the mother plant to be female. Take out clones and plant them in a separate grow pot. As they begin to grow green, the plants start taking form and grow in evenly along the wire mesh, thereby creating a form of a canopy.

This is why it called a screen of greens. When you look at it from the screen, it is not only beautiful to see, but in perfect condition. As the screen helps redirect light from the weak fluorescent, the plants grow more healthy, strong, and full.

4. Light Bending: It is pertinent to know that many of the plants will not grow equally and at the same rate. As a matter of fact, some will continuously grow faster and toward the direction of the light, thereby, receiving more light at the expense of others in the grow room.

If this happens, what should you do? It simple. Make sure you always adjust the light to suit the rest of the plants. If you change the direction of the light, other plants will be able to absorb more light than before, thereby fostering their own growth too. Also, if the plants continuously start bending toward the light, it will grow outside the pot and get heavy, especially when it starts producing buds.

This one-sided growth would definitely sway the weight of the pot to one side, thereby falling the pot as time goes on. Switch the plants if possible - and if they can't be interchanged, then tie the bent plants up until they learn to remain upright.

How badly do you want to multiply your plants? How badly do you want to improve the qualities of your plants? With more than enough techniques available at your disposal, you shouldn't be complaining of a low yield and low-quality plants. Simply choose one and start applying it to your garden.

Chapter Six

Indoor Growing: Flowering Stage

The flowering stage of the indoor growing method of cannabis planting builds on the final phase of the plant. If you have reached this point with little or no qualms, then kudos to you. Pulling this off as a beginner is something to be proud of. The flowering phase signals the harvest period in all cannabis plants.

When you hear about flowers in cannabis, we are certainly not talking about the beautiful red rose or white lily kind of flower you can present to someone. Instead, we are referring to flowers that stink. Flowers that are beautiful, yet must be hidden from people because they may get you in trouble. Yes, those kinds of flowers.

It is important to know that the stench these flowers emits as regards their species and strains. They vary and some hold stronger scents than others. This is why we recommend you take precautions with the smell. Always ensure your grow room can take the smell perfectly without the aroma getting to leave the confines of the grow room.

The flowering phase comes only with the females. You don't expect the males to be sprouting out flowers, do you? So, if your plants have matured enough to sprout flowers but you aren't seeing any, then it's possible you have more males than females, or no females at all, in your garden.

How well do you know the cannabis plant? Let us make it clear. The males carry the pollen, do not put out flowers, and mostly focus on getting seeds. Thus, in order not to get mistaken or carried away, we would recommend you start removing the male plants in your garden as soon as you can.

This flowering stage is one of the most important stages in the life cycle of the cannabis plant. Notwithstanding, it is where we would advise you to pay more attention to your plant. It would be very painful if your plants got to this stage and eventually become useless.

The flowering stage can also be called the pregnancy stage in the cannabis plant. Look at it this way - the male plant possesses the pollen which is stored in the pollen sacks or even stored by the grower. Then, after a period of time, it empties this pollen sack full of pollen on the female plant.

The female plant, who will be patiently waiting for this process and pollen, would immediately produce white hairs along the internodes and top cola. These hairs are called pistils, which are produced in anticipation for these pollens. These pistils are sticky for the purpose of attracting more pollen to themselves when the male plant spreads it.

Now, relate this process to human reproduction. You

would agree with me that the processes are quite similar. The pollen in this vein would be the human sperm and the pistils would be the female eggs that are always ready to be fertilized by the sperm. The blooming flowers it would sprout afterward is representative of pregnancy.

Each strain or species comes with a different flowering time. Sometimes, the breeder's timing of the cannabis plant in flowering stage appears to be slightly different from what the plant brings out. For example, the breeder's instructions might predict the flowering stage to occur in the second to third month of growth, but the plant might go over that period of time by a week or two.

Changes that Come with the Indoor Flowering Stage

There is really no cause for alarm, as this happens frequently. The flowering stage marks the slow end of the vegetative stage of the plant. You don't expect the plant to be growing rapidly at this point. When the flower starts coming out, it means the plant has reached its peak, thus, signaling slow growth.

After absorbing the pollens from the male plant, the pistils, which are located at the top cola, will now begin to produce resins over time. However, the plant will continue to grow at a slow pace, with buds getting bigger, the stems and branches getting fuller, and the THC getting richer.

This formation will now make the plant take the shape of a Christmas tree. Additionally, the leaves at the bottom will start stretching out more so as to get enough light in the grow area. If it remained in the normal shape like before, it would definitely not get enough light from the fluorescent bulbs.

The tips of the leaves will start getting swollen. These swollen leaves will automatically trigger the change in color of the pistils from white to any color as specified by the breeder. The type of color it comes with is largely determined by strain or species of cannabis you are growing. Some strains or species change from white to orange, some to white to brown, and others change from white to red. As we said, it all varies.

The plants will start growing yellow leaves at some point. Make sure you pick these yellow leaves if you still haven't planned on harvesting. It is also the right time to start focusing on nutrients with a large portion of phosphorus and potassium ahead of nitrogen.

Like we pointed out above, the flowering stage is all about taking a closer look and giving closer attention to your plants. The phosphorus and potassium nutrients will help your plant during the flowering stage. Also, watch out for molds. They can be very harmful to your plant at this particular stage.

Be sure to use the ratio of 15: 30: 30 portion of the fertilizer, whereas nitrogen carries 15, phosphorus carries 30, and potassium carries 30. This is the right combination of fertilizer that is perfect for this stage. It will enable the plant to produce more resins it needs for this stage.

The flowering stage is all about preparing for the next stage of the plant, which is the harvest. It's all about how much you've cared for your plant thus far. It's all about how well your plant has grown over that period of time from its Vegetative Growth stage to the Flowering stage. It's all about knowing full-well that you are on the right track as regards growing cannabis.

It is important to know that darkness triggers the flowering stage here. Unlike the outdoor growing method, where everything takes place naturally, the indoor growing method can be influenced and tweaked by the breeder. If you set your light to at least a 10 to 12 hours of uninterrupted darkness, flowering will trigger.

If your garden loses light for that particular amount of time, the plants will stop trying to grow more and instead direct their focus in the massive production of buds. Switching off the light here triggers the flowering stage, and for a period of 7-9 weeks, these buds will continue to grow until you reach harvest. However, this timing may also differ as regards the different species and strains.

The flowers are a sign of a healthy plant. However,

growers of indoor cannabis plants tend to manipulate their plants' flowering stage. If it gets to a point where you feel your plants should have been bubbling with flowers at the top, then all you need do is give the plants more darkness than light. That should do the trick.

But, letting the plant grow out naturally is also great. That way, everything will grow out in the right timing. With that being said, the next chapter will open up your eyes on how to grow cannabis outdoors. It promises to be much more educative and informative. Don't forget to turn the page over.

Chapter Seven

Outdoor growing: Factors to Consider Before Starting

Growing marijuana at home is a fun and exciting experience that comes with a lot of rewards. But, when you decide to do this, you have to be patient, because this experience can be frustrating, expensive and very challenging - especially if you are a first-time grower. Opting for outdoor growing is advised, especially if you have limited resources and you are first time grower or you just love the lovely aroma and flavor of outdoor-grown cannabis.

Before starting an outdoor cannabis garden, you need to understand what you are going into. Some people are quick to opt for indoor growing because of environmental and weather control, but indoor growing poses to be very expensive, especially for medical reasons or a first timer with limited resources.

Anyway, if you choose to stick with outdoor growing, without putting in a large monetary investment, you can yield a lot of good old cannabis from even the smallest outdoor garden. Some of the major advantages of outdoor growing include the unlimited vertical and horizontal space to grow, a healthy organically-grown marijuana (some people believe cannabis that is grown indoors are not sun-fed or organic), a unique flavor and aroma that is very satisfying.

It only comes with outdoor growing and many people prefer this, especially for medical reasons. To start this exciting and interesting journey of growing your own cannabis outdoors, all you need is access to a sunny spot on the rooftop, a terrace, a balcony, or even a large private yard.

Going further in this chapter, we will be making your journey to a successful outdoor garden easy by explaining some major factors to consider when starting an outdoor cannabis garden.

1. **Climate:** It is crucial to understand how the climate works in the area where you live, as this can help you understand how to control the growth of your cannabis and protect it from harsh conditions. Though cannabis is very adaptable to many climate conditions, it is susceptible to extreme climates.

A temperature that is above 86°F can cause your cannabis plants to stop growing, while temperatures below 55°F can cause your plant damage and even death. In the case of heavy rain or heavy wind, your plant faces a threat of physical damage. Also, molds and powdery mildew are likely to nest on your plant, especially if it's moist, so you have to be extremely careful.

In such cases, it is advised to grow your plant in a container outdoors so it can be moved easily during harsh weather conditions. You also need to understand the length of day and night and its changes seasonally in the area where you live. In some places, you get 14 hours straight each day; in others, you can get 16 hours straight.

2. Location: Before jumping into the strain you want to grow, you have to find an appropriate location to grow your plant. This is the most important decision you have to make, especially if you are thinking of planting on the ground or inside an immobile container or pot. There are a number of factors that influence this decision.

The first factor that affects the decision of location is climate, which we have already covered. But, in addition, if you are looking to start an immobile garden, then you should choose a spot that gets direct light and a good amount of early morning sun and filtered sun during the mid-day (the hottest time of day). Basically, your plant should receive the least of 5 to 6 hours of direct sun per day.

You should also check for a spot that is a little breezy, especially in a hot climate location. Though this can cause your plant to consume more water, I am sure you can handle that. Well, on the other hand, if you are living in an area that experiences high winds, it is advised to plant your cannabis near a fence, a large shrub, or a wall. In other words, plant near some sort of windbreak.

If you live in cool climate areas, then it is wise to plant in a spot that can retain heat like near a fence or brick wall facing south. For hot climate residents, what you need do is avoid these kinds of spots.

Another factor that influences the decision of location is choosing a place that provides shelter to your cannabis plants in harsh conditions like strong rain and wind or a cover for your plant at night. In this case, you should consider growing your plant in a pseudo-outdoor space like a greenhouse.

A third factor that influences the location of a cannabis garden is security and privacy. You have to protect your plant from thieves and judgmental neighbors, especially if your garden is not located in an isolated area. It is advisable to build tall fences and plant large shrubs and trees to protect your garden.

Other safe locations you should consider include planting in a mobile pot or container in rooftops or balconies, out of sight of thieves and neighbors. Some people even go as far as building heavy cages to keep out thieves and animals. Anyway, it all depends on your choice. Before you make any choice though, take into consideration that the cannabis plant can grow up to 15 feet, so you should definitely plan accordingly.

3. **Soil:** There are three major types of soils you can choose from which are clay, silt, and sand. For successful cultivation of cannabis and for your yield to thrive, your marijuana needs to be planted in a soil rich in organic matter that is well drained and very slightly acidic.

So if you choose to plant directly on the ground, you need to study and understand your soil composition and amend it accordingly to benefit your plant. So when you are choosing a soil, here are some factors you should consider.

Clay soils don't hold oxygen and drain at a slow pace. If this is the kind of soil you are working with, then serious amendments need to be made. To provide this kind of soil with nutrients, easy and fast drainage, and aeration that is beneficial to your plant, all you have to do is dig holes large enough to fit your cannabis plant and pour in a mixture of compost organic matters like worm castings, composts and manure a month before you start proper planting.

Sand soils, on the other hand, are quite easy to work with. They drain fast and well, but can't hold nutrients well, especially in environments that see a lot of rain. This is because sandy soil is so loose that water and rain can easily wash out the nutrients. To amend this, you will also dig large holes where you expect to plant your cannabis, and pour in a mixture of compost, coco coir, and peat moss.

What this does is bind the soil together and provide it with air circulation and food. Furthermore, to avoid your soil getting too hot, hence affecting the roots of your plants, sandy soil is advised to be mulched to help with water retention.

Finally, **silt soil** is considered the best medium for growing cannabis. This type of soil is easy to work with, holds moisture, warms quickly, contains lots of nutrients, and has good drainage. This type of soil is considered the most fertile and doesn't need much amendment.

So basically, before you start your cannabis growing, it is essential to test the soil you are about to use. There are many testing services you can engage in that provide you with vital knowledge like the acidity and alkalinity of the soil and the kind of amendments to carry out. They are also inexpensive.

4. **Seed:** Having chosen the right spot and established an appropriate soil for planting, the next thing to get into is the seed to be planted. Here, you have to be able to distinguish the different types of seed and how well they will thrive within the climate of your location and the soil you are planning to use. These seeds fall into two categories, Sativa and Indica.

The first thing to consider when picking out a seed is

harvest month. The ability to know harvest months helps you determine the right time to start germination. It is important to keep in mind that harvesting after October is a definite no-go, because this will just be an invitation for molds, being a period of excess humidity.

The second factor to consider is the growing traits of the seeds you are planning to use. Strains dominated by Indica can thrive well in cold and harsh conditions. On the other hand, Sativa-dominant strains thrive well in hot and humid conditions. Note also that harvesting Sativa takes longer because of the added weeks it takes for it to complete its flowering phase.

5. **Germination:** Here, you have to decide whether you want to germinate your seed (with a specific germination method) or directly plant them in the soil. If you choose to plant directly in the soil, then you won't have to worry about eventually transplanting seedlings later on. If you choose to germinate, below are two methods you can consider using.

For the first method, you place the seeds in water for 24 hours. This process will encourage your seed to germinate before planting.

The second method involves using two sheets of moist paper towel. It has to do with placing the seeds in between the paper towels. Afterward, leave this in a dark, warm room for a few days until you sight taproot germinating from the seed. After this, transfer your seedling into the soil.

6. **Fertilizer:** Over the long life cycle of cannabis, they require a good amount of food, especially from Nitrogen, Phosphorus and Potassium, popularly known as NPK. There are some effective methods to consider when feeding your plants. These include:

The use of **commercial fertilizers** is effective and can help improve your yield, but this method is advised to be used by an experienced grower. Nutrient solutions made specifically for the growth of cannabis can be purchased from local grow shops. You should be careful how you use this on your cannabis plant as they can damage your soil because of its high composed synthetic alkaline that is meant to be used for indoor growing.

You can decide to opt for a more **organic fertilizer**. This method of fertilization is a good option, as it minimizes the harm in the soil and uses the microbial life in the soil to its full advantage. Organic fertilizers can be easily found in local home and grow stores. Some of these fertilizers are blood meals, bat guano, kelp meal, fish meal, and bone meal.

The final method of fertilization that is used these days has to do with the use of **organic pre-fertilized soil**, or Super Soil, as it is popularly known. This fertilizer can be homemade or bought from a local store. Just dig a hole for your cannabis plant, fill it halfway with Super Soil and fill the top half with potting soil.

7. **Maintaining your Plant:** At this point, everything is already up and running. Your energy should be focused on providing a smooth growing period for your plants. This is when the most important work comes in. One major activity to be done in this period is watering your plant.

8. **Watering:** Watering is very important and essential to the growth of your plant, especially outdoors. You have to be delicate when watering your plants because it is very easy to overwater your plant. So, always check the moisture level of the soil before watering your plants. In other words, wait until the soil becomes dry before you water.

Hence, if it's rainy season, be sure to always drain your garden regularly. Also, be careful about the kind of water you use to water your plant. Note that cannabis requires soil with a pH of 7 (neutral) to thrive. So be sure to use water that will not affect this pH of the soil. Just like fertilizers, overdoing it can end up killing your plant.

9. **Protecting Your Cannabis Plant:** One of the major problems cannabis plants faces, especially in outdoor

gardens, is physical and natural threats. You have to be extremely careful in order to provide protection for your plants.

Physical threats include threats from insects and large animals. In this situation, there are organic pesticides and insecticides you can use to control pests. To control large animals, you can use fences and chicken wire to build gates and protectors for your garden.

The **natural threats** have to do with uncontrolled environmental factors like droughts, rain, wind conditions, and temperature changes. Solutions to handle some of these issues have been mentioned above. Additionally, though, you have to learn about these threats and challenges so you will be able to tackle them.

Growing outdoors is a very fun and interesting experience - and you get to learn a lot along the way. Just be sure to always keep an eye on your plant to prevent unwanted problems. Anyway, enjoy this experience and we'll see you in the next chapter.

Chapter Eight

Outdoor Growing: Planting Technique and Propagation

Believe it or not, propagation and planting techniques are vital toward maintaining a great garden of weed. Have you ever thought of how you could replicate your small number of plants or seeds into something much more plentiful? Instead of spending a lot buying expensive seeds of the same species and strain, why not just make use of simple propagation and planting techniques?

Propagation here has to do with the breeding of a plant specimen naturally from its parent stock. In the case of growing cannabis, propagation is an art that can be divided into two major sets of skill. These skills are:

1. The skill that deals with replicating genetics you have.

2. The skill of creating new genetics.

Furthermore, we will be discussing the approaches you can use to create new plants and how to care for them. Going further, there are two major approaches you need to know for starting a new weed plant. This is growing from seeds and growing from clones.

SEED

A seed is simply an embryo, so to speak. It is typically a tiny plant that gradually grows to become a large structure. This process of growing new plants from seeds is a situation where the male pollen cannabis plants pollinate the organs of your female cannabis plants.

When you provide the right conditions for your seed, it is likely to prosper and grow into a full-grown plant. In considering the best conditions for your plant, you have to take note of soil, humidity, and temperature.

To successfully choose your male and female cannabis plants for sex, you have to be careful and use this biological means to make new variations for your marijuana plants. One more thing you should know about seeds is that they act just like human DNA. They are always unique from their parent plants. Unlike clones, which allow you to create an exact same plant with the exact same features.

CLONES

Cloning is also called vegetative propagation. This process deals with cutting a part of your existing plants to create new clones. Like when you are using seeds to create new plants, the clones also thrive better in the right conditions like good humidity, temperature, and soil. Under these good conditions, the part of the plant you cut will develop healthy new roots and develop into a new plant.

1. Growing a New Marijuana Plant from Seeds: If you are looking to grow totally new plants with unique DNA or just looking to experiment with your plants in different variations, then you should consider planting by seed. To get started, you can get marijuana seeds from a local grow shop/store or a seed bank close to you.

To plant these seeds, you have to use a sterile medium for planting that will prevent your plants from being affected by fungus. You should also make sure that whatever means you are using to plant should have enough room for your plant to enable the root of your plant spread out and grow freely.

In other words, if you are using a container or pot as a medium to grow your marijuana, then you should make sure the container or pot has enough room for your plant root to grow. Going further, germinate your seeds by soaking the seeds for 2 to 3 hours. In some cases, some people soak their seeds for 24 hours. When these seeds have soaked to your satisfaction, you will place them into the soil for planting.

At this point, there is no need for fertilizers. Just maintain a moist and warm environment for your plant. There should be gentle airflow into the soil and even distribution of daylight for your plants. Watering your plant is also very essential, but be careful not to overwater your plants - just make them moist.

After five days, your seed will start to pop out, and in two weeks' time, you will have a full blown plant. At this point, you can start using appropriate fertilizers to feed and enhance growth in your plants. After planting, keep away from checking the seeds you have already planted. This will only disrupt your plant's growth.

You should note that planting a marijuana seed is not like rocket science. It is very easy, just as planting other seeds in your garden. You just have to do proper research and be really delicate in dealing with a cannabis plant.

2. **Growing a New Cannabis Plant from Clones:** In cloning, the plants consist of undifferentiated cells that are called meristem cells. These meristems are so amazing that they can turn into flowers, roots and other parts of a plant. This allows a plant to create and grow new plants from a cutting.

When you choose the cloning method for creating new plants, these newly grown plants will be similar to their parent plant. Hence, the reason for the name "clones." This method is considered the most popular method to propagate a cannabis/marijuana plant because of its many advantages.

For instance, if you want your plant to have similar traits as its parent plant like effect, flowers, and gender, this method of cloning is the best for you to practice. Cloning generally sounds like a complicated fiction of science when it comes to humans and animals, but in the case of plants it's pretty easy to do.

What do You Need for closing?

1. Sharp razor blade

2. Small plastic or glass container/pot with a growing medium

3. Watering equipment for providing moisture for your plants, like a spray

4. Alcohol (application of alcohol)

Tips to Consider when Cloning Marijuana Plants

5. Check for the traits you like and would like to replicate before choosing a plant for cloning.

6. Reserve at least one mother plant, which will be very useful to grow new plants with already-known genetics.

7. Cutting plants for cloning is a very delicate act and you should use alcohol to sterilize your hands, razors, and cutting blocks before starting.

8. Before cutting down a parent plant for cloning, regularly water the mother plants for 2 or 3 days. This watering will help wash out nitrogen which will make growing new

plants easier.

9. Use distilled water for watering your growing medium. A good example of distilled water is coconut water, Oasis cubes, and Rockwool.

After cutting, be careful not to touch the cuttings. You should also note that certain conditions like environment, growing medium, and climate for planting clones or planting seeds is very similar. Since you are planting outdoors, always remember to also keep your plants under great conditions by providing them with moist soil, warmth, and a good space for sunlight/natural light with a reasonable amount of breeze.

Generally, good hygiene and patience are key to the success and growth of your cannabis. Having learned these two methods of propagation, I am sure when next you are trying to grow new plants, it will be very easy for you. Just stick to the guidelines and tips and you are sure to have a great result.

Chapter Nine

Outdoor Growing: Flowering Stage

The flowering stage in cannabis growing is the moment you have been waiting for; the time your hard work is being realized. It is one of the most important aspects of the cultivation of cannabis plants. The flowering stage has to do with the period when your plants start showing they are almost ready to use buds.

In the life cycle of cannabis growing, this particular stage is very important, and as a result, you should pay a lot of attention to your plants during this period. In this stage of cultivation, your plant will halt in its growth and start producing what is known as buds or flower.

The growth period of your cannabis plants depends on the type of strain you planted. The flowering periods of most cannabis strains last for 7 to 9 weeks. This period lasts a little longer if you are dealing with Sativa strains. Stages in this time frame of nine-weeks include the transitioning stage, producing first buds stage, the growth of the buds, ripening of the buds, and finally, harvest.

Similarly, other activities and timing of your plants during this stage is dependent on the type of strains you planted in the first place. So do not fret if your plant doesn't follow a defined schedule.

If you are using the outdoor method to grow your plants, this flowering period will occur at the end of the summer, just when the days get shorter and the nights longer. Also, local climate contributes largely to the flowering period.

This important stage in the life cycle of your plant comes in light because of the way you maintained and protected your plant in the vegetative period. Regular watering, feeding and an even supply of light and darkness will lead to a healthy flowering period.

If your plant is able to reach this period, then you have to be careful and not give room for mistakes and error. This is a very delicate stage in the life cycle of your plant; any slight error or mistake can cause your plants to produce lower yields.

Considerations during Transition from Vegetative to Flowering Stage

Once your plant starts transitioning from the vegetative stage to the flowering stage, you will start to notice visible changes in your plant. Here are a few tips to consider using in this situation:

1. Your plant should be pruned in the first two weeks of the flowering stage in order to trigger the hormones of your

cannabis plant.

2. Stake and trellis your plant in order to support the plant buds as they gradually develop.

3. Finally, feed your cannabis plant with the necessary and appropriate nutrients to enhance growth, and gradually avoid giving too much water to your plant.

These are the few steps you should consider before your plants get into the flowering stage. Going further in this chapter, we will discuss more the above steps and tips, the different flowering stages, how to care for your plants during this period, and what to expect during the flowering stage. This chapter will be divided into the week-by-week stage of the flowering period.

FLOWERING STAGE (WEEK-BY-WEEK)

The flowering stage begins with a gradual process. Your plants won't just stop growing immediately and then start flowering. In the first few weeks (1,2,3) you will witness a drastic growth spurt. This is an important note to consider, especially if you want to provide your plant with sufficient growth space and when it comes to properly feeding your plants.

FIRST WEEK (TRANSITIONING PERIOD)

This first week of flowering is the transition period for

your plant. Like I said before, this is the period in which your plant will see a considerable growth spurt. In some cases, plants can almost double themselves in this period. As a result of the rapid growth, this flowering phase is also referred to as the stretch phase.

In this period, you will notice that as your plants are growing in size and height and they will start producing new leaves, mostly at the top of the plant (main colas), to make them sturdier and stronger.

In this period, your plant will see an increased need for growing nutrients; feed your plants with this nutrient for about a week when flowering starts before changing the nutrient schedule from growing nutrients to flowering nutrients.

Many growers tend to bend their cannabis plants in this stage of flowering in order to manage space. That is changing it from its original Christmas-tree-like shape to a horizontal-table-looking tree.

One important tip you should learn to practice in this period is, if you are cutting, be sure to avoid cutting off branches and leaves. At this point, your cannabis plant needs all the power and energy it can get, and cutting down these leaves will only make your plants weaker. In other words, always give your plant time and peace to grow and fully develop before use.

WEEK TWO

This is the time you will start noticing your female cannabis plant produces fine, white hairs where big leaves meet the main stems. These white hairs are what will eventually become buds. At this point, they are called white pistils. These hairs do not grow on male cannabis plants, which grow small pollen sacs instead.

This is the period when you should sex your plants and separate the females from the males, especially if you didn't know the gender of your plants before. It is important to separate your plants, or else the males will pollinate the females and make them produce seed - which is something you do not want to happen.

It is usually this time in the second week when you will need to adjust your plant's feeding schedule and increase flowering nutrients to increase high yield potentials.

WEEK THREE

In this week, your cannabis plant will still be growing and will be about 45% bigger than it was a few weeks back. It is now that your plant will gradually slow down its stretching (rapid growth) and eventually come to a halt and the white pistils on the female plants will start to turn to real buds.

Though the plant is growing well in this period, the sweet aroma of cannabis will still be mild and not very pungent yet.

It is in this phase of flowering that your plant will start putting in more energy to produce flowers. This phase is also very critical, so be careful and be sure to feed your plant with the appropriate dosage of nutrients as recommended.

Be sure to also watch out for potential deficiencies that could attack your plants in this period, like yellowing or discolored leaves, loss of leaves, and overfeeding (nutrient burns). One major signs of nutrient burns are that the tips of the plant leaves will start to discolor. At this point, you will have to reduce feeding your cannabis plant.

WEEK FOUR

In week four, growth or stretch would have already come to a halt in your cannabis plant. Your plants now will be focused on growing more buds that will be bigger and fatter with each passing day. It is at this phase of flowering your plants will start producing trichomes which help increase the aroma of your weed.

Since your plants have stopped growing in this period, you will have to provide good structural support for your plant. This could be by holding them up with, for example, a chicken net wire.

WEEK FIVE

In this week, you will notice the buds on your plants becoming much thicker than before. You will also notice new buds growing in new places like the main cola. With the growth of the buds on your plants, the size of your plant will increase every day. In this phase, the aroma of your plants becomes more pungent. It becomes a very intense odor, so ensure you have good ventilation to avoid problems, especially in regions that haven't legalized weed cultivation.

At this point, your plant is not far from being harvested. You will start to see signs like white pistils hairs becoming darker, turning to an amber or brownish color, and the hairs located and the trichomes turning milky white.

At this stage, most expert growers tend to trim their plant leaves to enable the plants to focus more on growing new and existing buds. This process is called defoliation. In doing this, you have to be extremely careful when trimming and be sure to leave enough leaves to support and promote your plant's health. The leaves help fuel the plant's system, hence increasing bud growth.

WEEK SIX, SEVEN, EIGHT (LATE FLOWERING STAGE)

As I mentioned earlier, the timing of flowering in cannabis cultivation is dependent on the variety of weed you planted in the first place. Not all the strains of cannabis require the same time frame for flowering. But generally, your cannabis plant will be ready for harvest in these last few weeks. This period will involve you flushing your cannabis and checking for the right time for harvest.

Flushing Cannabis

Flushing your cannabis plant is the situation where you stop feeding your cannabis plants with nutrients and you focus on administering plain old pH-balanced water to the plants. This process of flushing your cannabis plants will enable you to get rid of or flush out all the salt and minerals from the soil for purer and better tasting buds.

If you don't flush your cannabis plant, you may end up harvesting weed that is harsh and unpleasant, with a chemical taste. Flushing cannabis can be done two weeks before harvest of your plants.

Right Time for Harvest

At this point, your plants will be about ready to be harvested. You can use a small microscope or jeweler's loop to check the trichomes on your plants. In other words, before you jump into harvesting, you should check regularly whether the trichomes on your plant have turned from clear and transparent to a milky white color.

If the trichomes are still clear and transparent, then note that your plant is not ready to be harvested, so you have to wait a while. If, on the other hand, the trichomes reflect an opaque clarity or a beer color, then it's time for harvest. This is because, at this point, the THC content of the buds has reached its maximum and the plants are ready to be harvested.

The flowering stage is a very important part of cannabis growing. This is the period where your cannabis plant is most sensitive and delicate. Your plant will easily face some challenges and problems, but you shouldn't worry; there are always solutions to these problems. This is why your cannabis plant should be treated with caution and delicacy in order to avoid destruction to your plants.

At this point, harvest is around the corner and it is almost time for you to start enjoying your delicious cannabis/marijuana.

Chapter Ten

Natural or Human Pests in Marijuana

All good plants suffer from annoying little pests and predators. They are nothing but destructive agents that feed, mostly live, and even reproduce in the cannabis plant until they end up seeing the end of the plant (killing it off).

These pests or small predators eat up the vital parts of the plant little by little until it dies off completely. If we don't take the necessary measures in curbing this menace in our indoor and outdoor cannabis plants, we might end up losing every single one of them. When these pests and predators attack the plant, they make sure they leave nothing as they keep perching from one plant to another.

As a beginner, we would want you to keep in mind that these pests and predators will always be a problem, at least 80% of the time. Therefore, you should make sure they never turn your plants into their kingdom. Sometimes these pests and predators are so small that we might not notice them.

All of a sudden, we would realize that our plants are not growing as they should. We would realize that our plants are not drying off. And we would also realize that the leaves, pistils, branches, and many other parts are changing colors.

These are a few among the effects of these destructive pests and predators on our cannabis plants.

Only then would we realize that something is wrong with our plants. This is why cannabis growing should always be done with much attention and care. If you leave your plants carelessly, then be ready to get infested by these pests and predators. But, if you start caring for your plants from the inception until it's maturity stage, then there will be little or no pest problem.

With an outdoor weed growing pest problem, we would recommend you get a cat. Mind you, the cat is the number one defense mechanism you can ever use to flush out these predators of all forms. But with indoor plants, they can not be too trusted. As a matter of fact, they might end up bringing back pests into your garden. Thus, we strongly stand against it.

Here are the Natural pests you might find:

1. **Spider Mites:** The spider mite is one of the most deadly pests you will find in indoor plants. In fact, if you notice that your plants are infested with these pests, we would advise you to take precautionary measures as soon as possible because delay may be dangerous. They will leave your plants unhealthy and just a

caricature of the dream plants you've always had in mind.

What do they do? They enjoy liberty and freedom on the underside of your cannabis leaves and at the same time bore a hole through the plant cells in order to feed. The longer they stay on your plants, the deadlier they will become. Little by little, but at a fast rate, they will suck the plant cells, thereby turning the leaves into gray colors before they finally turn yellow and fall off.

If you pay close attention to your plants, you will realize that the plants are finding it hard to even grow. They will, however, throw some hints your way signaling help. Make sure you stay focused. If you don't end up finding a permanent solution to these pests, they will suck off a plant and perch on another until the cycle continues all over again.

How to Control: Spider mites love dry environments and soil. There are also certain levels of humidity they will thrive in. As a beginner in this field, always ensure you don't provide them with such an environment. If necessary, you can flush them out during the vegetative growth stage with a forceful jet of water.

2. **White Fly:** These are the tiny, white insects you see around the plants, especially if you try shaking it. You will see that some very white, tiny flies will disperse

and come back again when the plants settle. Those are the deadly white flies we are talking about.

Do not think they look pretty in their all-white color, because they are as deadly as a spider mite. They contribute to the downfall of your plants in more than one way. What do they do? First of all, they make sure they suck off the cells, nutrients, and even juices that are found on the leaves.

They also go a long way in making the plants look very weak and fragile. This is not good for your plants. A healthy plant breeds a bumper harvest. Additionally, they help transfer diseases and infections from one plant to another within the shortest time. Being a pest is understandable, but being a carrier of diseases and infections makes it one of the deadliest pests you will find.

How to Control: The best way to control these annoying white flies is through biological means. The French Marigold (T. patula) is the most effective plant that ensures these whiteflies stay clear from your plants. Grow these French Marigolds around the cannabis plants, or even position its grow pots around that of the cannabis plant. That is the effective way of controlling them.

3. Fungus Gnats: If it was only the adult fungus gnats that perched on your plants, it would have been better, because they are not deadly in any way. But their larvae, which stay deep in your pot, are the real threat to your plant. Fungus gnats are mosquito-like insects that will cause more than enough damage to your grow room if you don't take the necessary precautions.

The larvae are little, shiny, worm-like insects that stay deep inside the soil, causing havoc from beneath. If we don't know this, we might be forced to start eradicating the adults we see around without knowing the real problem is actually beneath. What do the larvae do?

They feed on the plants via the root - both healthy and diseased root. This will damage the plants, seedlings, clones, and so much more from beneath. Plants end up getting infected by this pest as a result of wet soil and diseased roots. They want an environment where there are fungi and algae in the soil. Don't give them that.

How to control: What they want is soil with too much moisture; a place where they can fully develop and establish themselves. Don't let that happen. Don't let your soil get overly wet. You can place down traps like the yellow sticky trap. They will surely get attracted. You can also pour Diatomaceous Earth (DE) on the top of your soil as it will kill off any present larvae. We would also recommend you change the soil, if possible.

4. Molds: There are various types of mold, but the particular species that attacks the indoor garden is called the Botrytis. The botrytis just doesn't infest all cannabis plants; it has its own conditions before it invades. First, the weather surrounding the plant must be of high humidity and also it must have seen a sign of a food source in the plant before it begins to perch.

Botrytis can only feed on your plants through an opening; a breakage in a part, a bruised part, and so on. It is only then that they can start sucking the life out of your plant. If the necessary precaution is not taken almost immediately, you might end up losing your plants. They may appear like trichome dust, but as time goes by, they will start changing color to gray with some hair-like spots around the flowers.

How to control: The best way to control this pest is to prevent it from occurring in the first place. Always check your plant regularly and see to it that it doesn't lack anything that would hinder its blossom. Also, remove and detach all broken parts from the pots. Do not drop them carelessly at the bottom of the plants. Any bruised parts should also be wrapped. You might be saving your plants from this pest in the long run.

Have you ever heard of a human pest before? Technically, you must have heard your friends calling each other pests. This doesn't mean they are giant walking insects with wings and all. It's just a literal word for anyone who bugs you frequently. This same meaning applies to this context of human pests relating to indoor cannabis plants.

Who are those people that may hinder or cause problems for you as you are growing your plants indoors? Who are those people you are scared of relating with when it comes to growing cannabis indoors? Those are the real human pests.

It is also natural for humans to want to claim bragging rights. For example, after harvesting your cannabis, you may decide to take some to your friends. No matter the sweet taste and high level of THC content in that weed, do not be tempted to open up. Your friends might start praising the grower with sugar-coated words. And like the humans that we are, we might be tempted to spill the beans and take the credit. This might feel good for a while, but not for long.

What if your friends betray you? What if they report you to the appropriate authorities? What if they even report to your landlord? Think about these questions first before doing anything that would make all your effort seem useless.

Here are some of the human pests you might encounter in your indoor growing of the cannabis plant;

1. **Authorities:** Imagine living in a place, region, or even country where all cannabis growers, users, and distributors are seen as scum. Where the law is ruthless as regards cannabis. Growing marijuana in this kind of

place would require absolute secrecy and topnotch security.

This is where the rule of "never tell anyone you are growing cannabis" comes into being. Even your trusted pals can tell on you in this case. Therefore, we would recommend you do the needful and ensure these human pests are well taken care of in case they come swinging by.

Your grow room should be very far from the other rooms. In fact, it should be very hard to locate for a stranger. That is the only way you will be safe if they come by. Keep to yourself in terms of growing cannabis, ensure your grow room is well-hidden, and enjoy absolute freedom from these annoying human pests.

2. **Landlord:** This can be quite annoying if you have a skeptical and traditional person as your landlord. If there is one person that has the right to inspect your house aside from the relevant authorities, then it is your landlord. First of all, he or she owns the building. Thus, if he or she finds or hear anything from anyone, the landlord can choose to carry out his or her own inspection.

Aside from that, he or she has no right to enter your home without prior notice. Like we said above, the grow room should be well-hidden, but we all know the landlord is no stranger to his own building. Thus, in order to avoid this embarrassment, we advise you to seek out a marijuana-friendly landlord before you start growing.

Pests, either human or natural are just annoying. If they aren't taken care of adequately, they will just keep coming back over and over again. If a particular plant is infected in the midst of others, quickly remove that plant and check if others are also infected. Infections in the cannabis plant spread quickly.

Thus, we would recommend you grow different strains so as to be on the safe side. With that being said, daily maintenance of the crop becomes necessary, especially if it is in the flowering stage. For indoor plants, how well is the equipment functioning? How effective is the ventilation of your grow room? Get your answers to these questions and more in the coming chapter. You don't want to miss out.

Chapter Eleven

Nutrients, Maintenance, and the Soil in Marijuana

All healthy marijuana plants we see, either in our friends grow room or even pictures online, have gone through a thorough check, maintenance, and nourishment. You can't just expect your plants to grow well without any form of maintenance and additional nourishment. Even human beings need these maintenances and nourishment so as to live a good and prosperous life.

If a man doesn't eat well, sleep well, drink well, and do things well, he will definitely look weak, worn out, and malnourished. This same thing applies to plants. If a plant doesn't get enough air, enough water, enough sunlight, and even enough nutrients, it will grow weak and eventually die off.

This is the very reason we have emphasized the fact that growing marijuana is a hobby to be cherished. Before delving into it, be sure to make up your mind about entering this venture. Treat the plant as your bride. Take good care of it and you will enjoy a bumper harvest in the long run.

Aside from the many nutrients, the plants also need air, water, and light. If these three elements aren't available at the disposal of your plants, they will die off. Thus, your grow room should be greatly ventilated. The windows should be wide enough, but shouldn't be too transparent for people to see what is inside.

Aside from the natural air that comes in from the windows, you can also get some good old fans which will further give enough air to your grow room. You can attach one at the top of the grow room. Then, you can also attach another very close to the windows and doors. Sometimes, cannabis odors can be quite strong. The fans can also try to kill the smell in the best possible way.

It is better not to have your friends wonder at the kind of smell your house holds whenever they come to visit. No fragrance can overcome the stench of cannabis. cannabis smell will take over the air, and if care is not taken, may alert unwanted attention for the wrong set of people.

Get the best quality in terms of the fluorescent light in the grow room. You can't afford to go for something cheap and low quality. The light might end up not being bright enough, or even get damaged sooner than the quality ones. This would mean an additional cost to your pockets. Wouldn't it be wiser to buy the best one to begin with?

HPS Lamps are also good for the flowering stage. Although it might reach a point in the flowering stage where darkness would seem like a better option, the HPS Lamps will still provide your plants with enough support to successfully scale through that stage.

Always clean these lamps and fluorescents occasionally. Be sure to check their connections in order to avoid something crazy - fire, for example. And if you have any wireworks that need to be done, endeavor to do that before you plants start growing tall enough for the electrician to see through the window or perceive the smell. The last thing you would want is the authorities on your tail.

Don't forget to tweak the light so as not to cause unnecessary heat for the plant. If the temperature is too hot, the plant might end up getting fried. That is why we recommend you use the newly invented T5 Fluorescent which comes with little heat impact. It is very good for all species and strains of the cannabis plant.

Water should be applied to the plants occasionally. Don't allow the soil to be too damp. This is definitely not good for the plant. But instead, keep it moist at all time. Some soil is very good at holding water - far better than others. Thus, too much water is not advisable. You can also get a watering can or an automatic water sprinkler; it all depends on the level of your pocket. With these, you can easily water all the grow pots at the same time. It saves time and effort.

For outdoor maintenance of your weed farm, there are a lot of things to be done. Being that the plants are planted outside is something to consider while maintaining the farm. Outdoor cannabis farming is very tedious. Occasional weeding of unwanted plants is very necessary. Sometimes you can leave those plants so as to serve as a barricade for people.

If a weed is planted alongside plants of the same color, shape of leaves, and height, it is bound to leave confusion in the minds of people, except if one truly looks very closely. That is when you will be able to differentiate which is which.

The plants should have enough space between them, that way they can absorb more than enough light, water, and air altogether, instead, of one outgrowing the other. It is very possible for a plant in the outdoor farm to start outgrowing another. It is your duty to correct such growth so as to have an even rate of growth.

Maintenance doesn't just come with the plants alone; it entails the facility and equipment also. From the simple tweezers to the small spray bottle; from the grow pots to the grow room. Everything should be in the right order.

Nutrients

Most times, it not just all about the nutrients of the soil. Like, for example, a soil which was bought for outdoors might possess a very good quality of the NPK. But the question remains, how long can it stand without help from these sold or artificial nutrients? If a farmer wants to use pure naturally-sourced nutrients to boost his soil all through the period of growth, it's his choice and that is also very possible.

However, the work will be very tedious. He will have to start gathering natural nutrient boosters like dungs, compost, and so much more. This can be quite hectic in comparison to the easy nutrients pack you can get at the nearest store close to you.

Nitrogen, Phosphorus, and Potassium are the key nutrients to the success of growing cannabis. Each nutrient is very important to each stage of cannabis growth. The Nitrogen nutrient should be used more when the cannabis plant is in the Vegetative Growth stage. For the Flowering stage, the Phosphorus ratio should be more than the Potassium and Nitrogen. This will aid the plant in adjusting and passing through a successful Flowering stage.

They come in normal natural soil or as artificial soil sold in the form of fertilizers at an agricultural store. Their composition is mostly 60% of the nutrients and 40% of many other elements that make up the fertilizer. To this effect, their composition is at an equal level of NPK 20:20:20.

Aside from these key nutrients in the soil, there are also secondary supplements which aid the growth of the cannabis plant. Even if they are not as important as the NPK, they also contribute their quota to the successful growth of your weed garden. They include Calcium, Magnesium, and Sulphur.

There are also micronutrients which are not very important to the plants, but their presence is a blessing. They help in preparing the plant against external bodies, give it the vigor and hardiness it needs, and improve its quality. They are Iron, Boron, Chloride, Manganese, Copper, Zinc, and Molybdenum.

If you are really looking to boost your yields, we would advise you get yourself a very good fertilizer and know exactly when to apply them or what exact quantity of nutrients one should apply. We would recommend you get quality fertilizers, like Miracle-Gro, for example. This fertilizer has the tendency to ensure your plants grow faster and healthier.

The Soil

Without this, the seeds might germinate, but they won't grow. The soil gives them the support with which they pitch their roots. It provides the support the plant needs to stand upright and strong. So, when we tell you that the soil is a very important part of growing cannabis, please believe us.

There is more than one soil type you can choose from. If one doesn't suit your style, then you opt for another. There is the loamy soil, the sandy soil, the clay soil, and the humus soil.

These are the different components of soil which hold up the cannabis plant. But, the best among them in growing cannabis is the humus soil. It contains mostly compost materials, making it rich in nutrients.

With the humus soil, one would only need to buy the very little fertilizer. It can also be purchased at any gardening store nearby. Humus is the real deal, but might also contain worms, insects, and other disturbing insects. This is because it is the combination of compost and loam.

Humus holds water; thus, be careful with the water you spray on it. Be sure to check if the humus soil is still dampened by placing your hand on the soil. You will be able to feel the moisture. And if you can't, you should dig up a very small hole close to the plant. Be sure it is not too close so as not to hurt the plant, break off a root, or even create room for bugs and worms.

No plant will thrive if the grower doesn't maintain it. If the grower just sows the seeds and decides to leave the rest to nature, there will be no plant to harvest. Instead, either the plant gets ravaged by weeds, it gets destroyed by pests, harsh climatic conditions dry up the plant, or some other issue occurs.

To sum it up, the plants wouldn't survive at all. This is why there is a need for you as a grower to cater to, maintain, and even care for the plant until it reaches the harvest stage. How does one start harvesting the cannabis plant? Read on to our next chapter.

Chapter Twelve

Marijuana Harvest (Indoor and Outdoor Growing)

After all is said and done, we have reached the final stage, which you have been patiently waiting for the past three months or so. For you to reach this stage means that all the hard work you've put into the success of your cannabis plant had paid off. And we really commend you for that.

A lot of beginner growers would have given up somewhere along the line. Especially with all the problems they would definitely encounter in this process. Being your first time growing cannabis, there would definitely be mistakes you would make as you progress toward this stage. These mistakes are very normal.

It is better to have a staggering growth of the plants on your first trial than to quit all of a sudden after hitting a few stumbling blocks. The end result (harvest) is definitely rewarding. Imagine taking two steps forward or backward and voila, you have your weed. Instead of the long distance you would have to cover to get it from a distributor. That is simply enticing.

The feeling that you get to make your own weed can be

quite scintillating. If you reach this stage of harvesting the cannabis plant, then it shows you have followed and understood this Handbook to the letter.

Nevertheless, harvesting cannabis is simply an amazing feeling. If you happen to have a very healthy plant, your harvest will no doubt be bountiful. After passing through the Sowing stage to the Germination, the Vegetative Growth, and the Flowering stages, the Harvest stage comes next.

The amount of time you will spend on harvesting a whole farm depends on the method of growing you use. For example, you cannot start employing people to harvest your few pots of indoor plants. Even one person can pull that off perfectly. Indoor plants don't really need much presence while harvesting because of the limited space of the grow room. However, the outdoor method might need the help of more than two people, depending on the size of the farm.

The end result (harvest) might change your mind, if you'd planned on quitting after the first trial. You will realize that growing marijuana can be quite profitable either as a hobby or even a business venture. However, indoor commercial growers don't grow just a few crops. They grow cannabis indoors, but in a large quantity.

A medical marijuana company might have a grow room that is as big as hectares of land. Coupled with the fact that they are licensed to operate such a business venture, they also find it profitable. Now, you can't tell me just one person can handle all those plants when it comes to their harvest season.

Provisions would definitely be made for such activities. It is important to note that the plants would start showing different signs which will signal their harvest stage. Always pay close attention to the plants, especially when they are in their flowering stage. Some growers might even prefer leaving them even after they are ripe for harvest. It's all depends on the choice of the grower.

But, in a situation where you are too anxious to reap the fruits of your labor, then you can cut them down. Mind you, cutting down a marijuana plant is not as simple as cutting down normal plants. Cannabis plants are tall, full, and sometimes have many buds. You can't just use a machete or a cutlass to cut down the plants without making the necessary arrangements.

Ask yourself these questions:

1. **Are you ready to make your harvest?**

2. **Are the necessary arrangements already in place?**

3. **What's next after harvest?**

If your answers to all these relevant questions are a yes, then you should proceed to harvest your plants almost immediately.

How to Harvest Indoor Cannabis Plants

The harvesting procedure of indoor cannabis plants is quite similar to the outdoor, except for the fact that this harvest will be done directly from the inside. Instead of cutting down the plants outside like the outdoor growing, the plants are already conveniently located indoors, saving you time and energy.

First of all, check your plants carefully to ensure that all of them are truly ripe for harvest. If you remember correctly, we talked about how some plants grow more rapidly than others. Endeavor to check each section or pot to make sure you don't end up harvesting the ones that are not yet ripe alongside the ripe ones.

That way, you will be able to give more room and convenience to those unripe plants. This space will allow them to also thrive and even produce more resins, allow them to spread out fully with their leaves getting bigger and giving more strength to the stems for helping the plant stand upright.

After a careful check of the trichomes and other major signs, you can now proceed with your harvest. Swiftly and neatly cut down the plant from the bottom so as not to cause any damage to the other plants. Then, proceed by taking it to the cool room with no light or even fresh air. After this, you should hang it in an upside-down posture with the base pointing up and the top looking down.

Take a clipper and start clipping out as many leaves as possible. We would recommend you don't mix up the leaves when harvesting. Make sure you always start with the fan leaves. Clip out as many as possible. Then, proceed to the secondary leaves. They are even more potent than the fan leaves in regards to their level of THC.

Meanwhile, as you are cutting these leaves, do not dump them in the same pile. You might want to differentiate them now. Always remember to create a separate pile for each and every kind of leave you cut. After cutting the secondary leaves, then go for the trim.

The trim is small leaves located at the top of the plant with resins all over their body. In other words, they are mostly covered in resins. This is because they are always very close to the buds. The trim has a very high THC content. They are, no doubt, the most potent of all the leaves.

Now if you look at what you've done carefully, you will notice that you have 3 piles of weed. That is to say, you have 3 different kinds of weed at your disposal. The fan leaves are the lowest in THC; the secondary leaves are a little higher than the fan leaves; and the trim is just perfect.

However, some growers also make sure the buds don't go

to waste. They make sure the buds are also harvested separately. According to them, the buds hold the best part in the harvest of the cannabis plant. They believe the buds contain the highest level of THC one can ever get.

How to Harvest Outdoor Cannabis Plant

Just like the indoor plants, outdoor cannabis plants also follow the same process, except for the fact that they are not harvested from the outside. Outdoor plants are grown outside, thus making it a long process for growers of the plant each time they want to harvest their plants.

First of all, be sure to check that the plants are all ripe uniformly or if some sections got ripe before the others. That way, you will be able to know which plants are ready for harvest or which need a little time to thrive and produce more resins.

Endeavor to get a clean sheet, cloth, or even polythene, which you would spread on the ground. This is because we don't want your plants to sweep the ground while harvesting. Sand might change the taste of your plants, thus, the need for this sheet to be spread on the ground before harvest.

Mind you, harvesting cannabis outdoors is quite labor intensive. It comes with lots of hard work and strenuous effort which can be very tedious for just one person alone. Imagine one person trying to harvest 5 hectares of weed plants; it's simply suicidal. Get help from your friends, or even employ workers, if possible. It will make your work faster.

Especially if it's a Sativa species that grows more than 10 feet tall, how would you manage that on your own? Cut down the cannabis plant from the bottom and make sure they are neatly arranged on the sheet. Afterward, stylishly roll the sheet and the weed together so they can be transported to the cool room.

Like the indoor cannabis plant, the outdoor plant should also be hung upside down. But in this case, they should be cut down into bits due to the fullness and bushiness of the species outdoor plants normally comes in (mostly Sativa).

Get a clipper and start the same process we had explained above all over again. Differentiate the leaves as you cut them. The cool room should be extremely dark with no penetration of light. Light, no matter how little, might affect the potency and content of the THC.

Harvesting the cannabis plant is very different from the way other plants are harvested. Harvesting marijuana needs more care in order not to mess with the taste and potency of the THC. After harvest, you dry, then cure. It's another whole process entirely. Don't rush it. Take your time so as to get the best out of every leaf.

Have you ever heard of medical marijuana? How

marijuana found its way into modern day medicine? The next chapter is going to shed more light on that.

Chapter Thirteen

Medical Marijuana (How it All Began)

The walk through marijuana growing has been a very long one. The battle for its legitimacy or illegality has also been an up and down issue which has been and still is a trending topic in the whole wide world. Prior to the legalization of medical marijuana in many regions and states of the United States of America, the fight had not been an easy one.

What some people see as a harmful substance or herb is what others see as a road to scientific exploration and breakthrough. A lot of researchers have written quite a number of books and engaged in a lot of studies in regards to the medical side of marijuana, and each and every one of them has come to one conclusion; marijuana is medically potent.

Even in the age of antiquity, physicians and traditional doctors had capitalized on the effect of this plant in doing wonders in the lives of their patients. The cannabis plants had been discovered initially as a medical herb; a very potent one at that.

The history of marijuana as a whole started out as an old and ancient herb used before the times of the Old Greeks and Romans, down to their era, and even after their era. Physicians of such periods would occasionally mix other herbs, ointments, etc. with the cannabis plant to get effective and efficient medicine.

In our previous chapters, we laid emphasis on how the seeds of marijuana had been seen in old tombs and graves of ancient Chinese Emperors and in excavated areas of Siberia. According to history, marijuana which was also known as "Ma" was heavily used in the treatment of ailments and diseases during the Old Chinese era.

As a matter of fact, it had been very expensive due to its high demand and potency. According to a well-renowned botanist Hui-lin Li, in China, "The use of Cannabis in medicine was probably a very early development. Since ancient humans used hemp seed as food, it was quite natural for them to also discover the medicinal properties of the plant."

The Chinese had been the first people to utilize the numerous properties and uses of the plant and its seed. During this ancient age, the Chinese had discovered quite a lot of things with the marijuana plant and seeds. For example, Hua Tuo, who was a surgeon in this era, had discovered how to use the marijuana plant for anesthesia. He had done this by grinding the plant into a powder, then adding it to wine. This is given to the patient before surgery.

The roots were used to eliminate blood clots and its juice was used to fight tapeworm. China can be said to have been more advanced medically than any other tribe, nation, or entity during that period of time. To them, every part of the plant was vital. From the top to the bottom, from the leaves to the root, from the flowers to the stems. Every part was - and is - useful.

Aside from the Chinese, many other kingdoms and empires at that particular time had also followed the trend of using cannabis medically to treat ailments and diseases. From the Old Greek settings to the Roman Empire, from the Ancient Netherlands to Ancient Egypt, from Ancient India to the Medieval Islamic world - they had all benefited from the medical benefits of marijuana.

Now, ask yourselves this vital question. If these ancient empires and kingdoms had seen the good properties attached to the cannabis plant, and at the same time benefitted from these outstanding qualities, why should we not also benefit from the same plant? As a matter of fact, we ought to even enjoy these properties more with the many sophisticated inventions and ideas of today's world.

With that being said, the road to medical marijuana didn't start today. Following the historical background of how it all began, you will agree with me that there is a lot to gain from marijuana if it was being legalized and not criminalized. To a large extent, lots of people might abuse this plant. But that can be curbed.

Before the criminalization of the plant, the 19th century ushered in a new phase in Western Medicine. It was now being used for therapeutic purposes. For instance, synthetic THC was invented in the form of a capsule with the brand name, Miranol.

Please note that the creation of this synthetic drug didn't in any way deter or regress the use of the plant via smoking. It's effect still remained the same whether you take it as a drug or you smoke it as a weed. According to its users, they believe smoking proves to be faster in showing its effectiveness.

Thus, cannabis drug manufacturing companies quadrupled in the 19th century. With over 2000 medicines being sold, each had at least a pinch of marijuana. Gradually, marijuana became the secret ingredient of most drug companies out there. They realized the versatility of marijuana in fighting different ailments and diseases.

Marijuana during this century started declining in medicinal use with the invention of injectable medical substances and aspirins. Injection became more rampant and also the popular choice amongst ailing persons.

Meanwhile, marijuana had been very helpful in curing and putting an end to lots of diseases. This is the driving force and point of people fighting for its legalization. They believe that if marijuana is made legal, it would save the government lots of revenue, create jobs for people, and be a solution to lots of trending ailments and diseases.

To be frank, the scientific explanation given of the properties of the plant is enough for one to do a rethink about either supporting its legalization or criminalization. On one hand lies the wonderful medical and scientific feats the plant would achieve if researchers were allowed to make quality research and findings. On the other hand lies the abuse, addiction, and menace it has caused in the lives of our youths.

At the end of it all, medical marijuana is a clean genre of cannabis utilization. It is strictly of the progress and further development of humanity as regards medical and health care. With lots of laws and edicts that had been promulgated over the years (Marijuana Tax Act in 1937, Enactment of the Boggs in 1951, and the Narcotic Control Act in 1956), legalizing cannabis has not always been an easy route to follow.

However, the light started shining on the path towards its nationwide acceptance when California broke the restriction jinx and legalized the medical use of cannabis in 1996. This was to be grown, harvested, and processed under strict supervision. The law was passed under the Compassionate Use Act, thereby giving license to just medical cannabis under the watchful eyes of the authorities.

Even if this was a restricted and limited victory on the fight against cannabis criminalization, it still counts for something. As a matter of fact, it gave the advocates the much-needed strength to pitch their voice even higher until it reaches every necessary nook and cranny of the United States.

On the 1st of January 2017, an additional 28 states also approved and passed into law the legalization of the cannabis plant within their jurisdiction. Growers of the cannabis plant can now grow, sell, distribute, and even buy the cannabis plant freely without any fear of intimidation or committing an offense.

Ever since, researchers and scientists have delved into the uses and properties of the cannabis plant, effortlessly trying to bring out the best of the plant in making the world a better place. Believe it or not, the marijuana plant has so far contributed its own quota to the development of modern-day medicine.

Marijuana is now being used to treat lots of diseases like epilepsy, cancer, HIV/AIDS, schizophrenia, and so much more. Now think of it this way, if marijuana hadn't been made legal or even studied at a particular point in time, would it have been this useful medically? The answer is no. Also, if people still see this plant as something deadly and harmful, then it is about time they change that perception.

This is because the plant has proven to be useful medically. Thus, it's about time we see the cannabis plant exactly the way it is; a plant full of medical possibilities. A plant with many medicinal uses, and a blessing to mankind.

Thank God for medical marijuana in today's world. There has been a massive improvement in the field of medicine as regards curing and reducing the effects of deadly diseases to the minimal. Right from inception, marijuana has been a blessing to man with its highly medicinal purposes, with ancient empires and kingdoms putting it to good use. That is how much marijuana has been shown to be a savior to our world.

The next chapter will lay emphasis on the success rates of medical marijuana in our world today and how important it has been after it's legalization. Flip the page over, will you?

Chapter Fourteen

Medical Marijuana (Exploration and Break-Through)

Exploring medical marijuana was another whole new perspective entirely. An interesting adventure, many would agree, especially for those who would want to explore it for the sake of science. When the crusade against marijuana as a whole gained momentum, it shot its exploration and breakthrough into the world of medicine many steps backward.

The period of time that could have served as the best time for its exploration and breakthroughs was used to fight laws and edicts levied against cannabis use and growth. If at this period of time, cannabis had been made legal, we would have advanced medically with cannabis beyond where we are currently.

A lot of medical companies have reignited their passion and drive toward cannabis growing for medical purposes. Legalizing cannabis can be said to have been one of the best decisions made by the country so far with lots of breakthroughs. A lot of people are now free to carry out well-detailed experiments and research.

The benefits of this research and the many experiments

have been felt in the world of medicine. By now, we are sure you are quite familiar with cannabis and its benefits, but do you know what it means medically? Instead of seeing marijuana as simply a psychoactive substance taken for the sake of lifting depression, we should cultivate the mind of seeing past this barricade. marijuana is far more than that.

Medically, it is one of the superior plants available on the planet. Its uses surpass those of many other plants. Even though research is still being carried out as to in which other medicinal uses the cannabis plant can be beneficial to us, it is important to know that the plant still serves more than enough purposes.

When we hear the term "medical marijuana" in the modern world, our mind often races down to the synthetic use of the plant. For example, when marijuana is added to other content to create a well-packaged drug or medicine. Our mind often drifts to capsules and tonics with marijuana content. Thereby, we start forgetting that even the traditional way of taking in marijuana as a medication is also vital, so long as it performs its functions clearly.

You can start saying that well-blended leaves of marijuana added to olive oil for a certain medicinal purpose is not acceptable as modern medicine. Surely, it lacks the branding and packaging these capsules and tonics come in, but it is as effective as the others, if not more effective.

The beginning of cannabis exploration can be said to have started in the 19th century when the cannabis plant was imbibed into the therapeutic side of medicine. Since then, they had remained in the limelight, even after the law was passed for its criminalization. One way or the other, the advocates of the plants still maintained a strong voice on the positive benefit it had contributed to medicine.

Today, millions of people have been treated using marijuana. It had become a very strong medicine used in curing and suppressing lots of ailments and symptoms. That aside, taking in marijuana for recreational purposes might just end up being the best thing you need for your health without even having the slightest idea.

The idea you portray to people when smoking cannabis in areas where it is prohibited can be quite bad. This is, no doubt, as a result of the stereotype maintained over time. But that apart, you are indirectly curing yourself or suppressing disease within you unknowingly. That is the power marijuana holds.

Be that as it may, modern-day researchers, scientists, and the pharmaceutical industry have continuously been striving hard to maximize marijuana as regards medicine. And yes, they have made a lot of breakthrough ever since the crusade started.

Breakthroughs

1. Recently, there has been a new development in the line of epilepsy treatment. A group of researchers, scientists, and pharmaceuticals companies had taken it upon themselves to create a solution to frequent epileptic seizures in people. This drug was called Epidiolex and was simply the purest you can ever find in terms of cannabidiol (CBD), a psychoactive substance inherent in the marijuana.

   With Epidiolex, it doesn't matter if you are epileptic from childhood or are suffering from a severe condition. It would ensure it reduces the seizures to the barest you can ever think of. This is one hell of a breakthrough.

2. Another form of breakthrough achieved by the invention and creation of medical marijuana is the steady increase in the life expectancy of people suffering from Glioblastoma Multiforme. This is a particular kind of brain cancer that is deadly and fatal with over 80 percent of its patients ending up dead. There is almost a zero percent chance of surviving this type of cancer.

   Initially, the life expectancy of this disease was just 2 years. However, GW Pharmaceuticals delved into medical cannabis with their research team and came out with a better panacea which will move the life expectancy of this fatal ailment with an additional 6 months. This is no doubt an important breakthrough in the field of medical cannabis.

3. Have you ever heard of Leukemia? No? How about cancer of the blood? Well, we are saying the same thing here. Leukemia is a very deadly type of cancer that attacks the blood cells. Nevertheless, a study was carried out recently at the University of London where it was proven that THC and CBD have the tendency to increase the effectiveness of the drugs against Leukemia.

   In the same vein, the result of the study shows that if you add both THC and CBD along with chemotherapy, the results are bound to be super impressive. Additionally, medical practitioners are now being advised to try out this new formula, which promises to be just perfect. With continuous research on this line, medical marijuana is bound to provide a lasting solution for Leukemia pretty soon.

4. Recently, Cannabis Science Inc., which is one of the strongholds of California's Biotech program, had gone into research and came out with an amazing feat in the field of medicine. The developed a process known as the Transdermal Patch to treat people suffering from Fibromyalgia.

   This Transdermal Patch is a pure medical marijuana process which involves the injection of equal parts of THC and CBD without patients having to smoke it or even inhale it. There is a considerable improvement in these patients over time as they now start exhibiting wonderful traits and responding to treatment. This company has also developed a cure for diabetic neuropathy via medical marijuana.

5. Although this study has not been carried out on humans yet, it was tested with mice by researchers in the University of Manitoba and the results were very positive. According to the research, CBD oil was tested on mice to see if it could help reduce or even stop the pains MS (Multiple Sclerosis) patients feel.

   This research was highly successful and the mice seem to survive and feel very little or no pain with MS. This could be one of the greatest achievement of all time as regards medical marijuana. Though studies and research are still going on, rest assured, they will definitely hit a breakthrough. And when they do, it's going to be a goodbye to MS pain.

6. The THC content in cannabis is one hell of a potent drug. It has also been discovered that this THC can be used to suppress and combat Alzheimer's disease. According to a study carried out by the Salk Institute for Biological Studies in California, it was discovered that the THC in cannabis goes a long way in serving the removal of amyloid, which is located in the brain.

   These amyloids can trigger the negative side of

Alzheimer's disease. The THC also helps reduce and relieve some of the inflammation located in the head. As of now, research is still being carried out as to how effective and how efficient the THC content in the cannabis plant could be in curbing the Alzheimer's disease.

Believe it or not, the legalization of cannabis in many states of the country has been a blessing more than it has been a curse. For example, when cannabis became legal again, people started seeing how harmful substances like opioids cannot alleviate them from depression, stress, worry, and emotional breakdown. Some medical practitioners now start prescribing marijuana as a medication for the cure of these setbacks we might feel.

Marijuana now took over from Oxycontin, Vicodin, and Percocet as their demand dropped drastically. According to research carried out by the Johns Hopkins Bloomberg School of Public Health, there is now a 25 percent drop in opioid consumption. What does this mean? It means states with legal marijuana now have fewer opioid in their streets and there is also a very considerable drop in the rate of opioid addictions.

Judging from these amazing feats marijuana has brought to mankind via medicine, would it still be wise to judge the beneficial herb with its demeaning stereotype? The answer is no. It's only a matter of time before researchers and scientists find a permanent solution to deadly diseases like HIV/AIDS via marijuana.

Our next chapter is the last chapter, which puts the lid on the bottle of our knowledge on cannabis with this amazing book. Don't let anyone discourage you from growing what you love. Take the bull by the horns and excel in growing this medicinal plant. You will be amazed at how you will move from a novice to an expert.

Chapter Fifteen

From Beginner to Expert Grower (It's That Easy)

Sadly, this is the end of the road for us as our journey together is going to end with this last chapter. If you have been following closely, then starting up a small cannabis garden of your own shouldn't be hard to pull off, either indoors or even outdoors.

Don't forget what we discussed if you find yourself in one of these countries or regions which criminalizes cannabis. You wouldn't want to get into trouble for doing what you love doing, right? Stay calm and look for a better place to grow your plants quietly, without unnecessary intervention.

Follow the steps in this Handbook attentively. Do not miss a step, or else you might end up mixing up everything as a whole. Don't let anyone discourage you. Even if you make a mistake, you can always correct your steps back. For example, if you end up pouring too much water in the case of an indoor plant, you can basically bore small holes around the pot to sieve out the water or just transplant it in another soil.

Water shouldn't be too heavy. The soil should be moist but definitely not wet. Additionally, as it's our first time growing cannabis, we just end up getting too anxious as soon as we plan the seed. We begin to count days until it germinates. And if it past the number of days written on the pack by the breeder, we now start panicking.

How do I know this? I've also been there. I've been in that position many years back. My first trial of growing cannabis was full of drama, suspense, and expectations. I'd expected my seeds to germinate in the first few days after planting. I would always assure myself that I'd followed every step correctly and perfectly as written on the internet.

The normal time passed and my seeds were far from germinating. Then I started seeing myself as a failed cannabis grower. At my first trial, I blew it. Thoughts started going through my mind. Was the water too much? Were the seeds buried too deep? Were the seeds even that great?

I'd almost given up hope when a few of the seeds started sprouting seedlings. I could swear that I was the happiest man alive at that particular moment. Now, that is the kind of feeling growing cannabis will give to you as you start as a beginner. But rest assured, the end result is all worth it.

Don't forget that every phase is very important. Although, many will say that the flowering stage is the most sensitive stage and one needs to be more attentive to the plants. However, all stages are as important - from the sowing to the germination, down to the vegetative and flowering stage.

You will surely witness problems and obstacles along the line. From natural to human pests, security, and so much more. It may even get to a point that you will become very tired and wouldn't mind giving it all up. You're surely not a quitter, are you?

Always make sure everything is in check, from the sowing stage, down to the germination, then the vegetative and flowering stage. And if you are growing in larger quantities as a beginner, then it's obvious you have the capital to fund it. Security should be the first thing to ensure in this case.

It would be a very big loss on your part if your enormous grow room or outdoor cannabis farm was raided and shut down by the relevant authorities. What necessary measures have you put in place to keep even the tiniest mice from entering your farm or grow room? In cases where your landlord pays you an unexpected visit, what would you do or what measures have you put in place to make sure he or she doesn't suspect a thing?

These and more are questions we should really ask ourselves. Moving from a beginner to an expert grower doesn't just happen out of the blue. You become an expert grower only if you continue growing the plants year in and year out until you become a pro in it.

Expert growers are professionals in the field of growing

cannabis. They are growers that have moved up the ladder of growing cannabis after attaining a certain level of perfection in the art of growing the plant.

But rest assured, anyone can attain this level. What matters is how much you really want to grow cannabis. Expert growing is far beyond burying cannabis seeds and forgetting to dig them back up. As an expert grower, even when sowing the seeds, there are rules to follow. Rules like not sowing the seeds too deep, rules like giving a considerable spacing between the seeds, and rules like watering and tending to the seeds until the germinate.

You can also try out new ideas and techniques if you want. Don't be scared to explore with your plants. You might end up breeding a new strain which is unique from the rest. Mind you, this is how breeders start creating hybrids. As a matter of fact, one might not be entirely wrong if he or she sees the first ever hybrid created as a mistake of the grower.

With time, you can also develop your own hybrids. Don't forget to hype the soil nutrients. Sometimes, natural soil nutrients just aren't enough. You need to buy artificial soil or even a rich fertilizer that contains Nitrogen, Phosphorus, and Potassium (NPK).

These additional nutrients will boost the quality and quantity of your plants. They would ensure your plants come out perfectly fine and with an outstanding taste. This is one of the secrets every grower of the cannabis plant relies on. You can also choose to go for natural fertilizers. For example, you can create compost and feed that to your cannabis plants. Compost is also a great source of fertilizer for your plants.

Lastly, remember that cultivating and harvesting the cannabis plant takes courage and guts to pull off successfully. It's more than just a hobby. It should be taken as seriously as one's passion, one's new bride, and one's business venture.

Conclusion

Alas! We have arrived at the final point where we would say a very big thank you for sticking with us all through this interesting and amazing experience. No doubt, your perspective and conception of the stereotypes surrounding the cannabis plant must have shifted to a better paradigm of the plant.

Moving from a novice grower to an expert one is no small feat. It is not an easy road, but with time, you will get there. Rome wasn't built in one day. It takes time before something great comes into being. Thus, do not feel bad each time your effort to grow good crops turns out bad.

In becoming an expert grower, one would have to be constantly trying to grow cannabis. You would have to be trying out new strains, new strategies, new techniques, and new processes. It doesn't matter if you fail constantly. What matters is you will keep trying.

Nevertheless, be confident in yourself. Be sure to always refer back to this book anytime you feel stuck. You can also surf the internet for more ideas if that will make you feel better. Don't forget to equip yourself with everything you need, especially if you are venturing into the indoor cannabis growing method.

Your pocket weight should determine which method you would want to go for. If your budget is considerably low or below average, then it's obvious you won't be able to maintain the indoor method of growing. How would you pay for lighting? How would you pay for the fans? How would you pay for the fertilizers? These are questions that will pop up with time.

How will you take care of all that if you don't have money? Thus, do not burden yourself with unnecessary stress. If you are not well equipped financially for it, then switch to the other option - the outdoor method of growing cannabis.

After reading this book, we are sure you would now serve as an agent and advocate of the plant. For instance, if you happen to see someone stereotyping the plant, won't you be glad to enlighten that person on the positive features it holds? Won't you take it upon yourself to correct and open the eyes of that person toward the benefits derived from the plant so far? Aside from teaching you how to grow the plant, this is also one of the goals of this book.

With that being said, we want you to go out there and start growing. Put everything this book had taught you to good use. Follow the steps and correct mistakes along the way when the need arises. Grow, grow, and grow until you become an expert in growing this plant.

Thank you and Bye for now!

***

www.ingramcontent.com/pod-product-compliance
Lightning Source LLC
Chambersburg PA
CBHW070951080526
44587CB00015B/2257